Homemade Business

Homemade Business

Donna Partow

Publishing
Colorado Springs, Colorado

Homemade Business

Copyright © 1992 by Donna Partow

Partow, Donna.
    Homemade business : a women's step by step guide to earning money at home / Donna Partow.
        p.   cm.
    Includes bibliographical references.
    ISBN 1-56179-043-5
    1. Home-based businesses—United States. 2. Women-owned business enterprises—United States.
3. New business enterprises—United States. 4. Work and family—United States. I. Title.
    HD2336.U5P37   1992   92-3753
    658′.041—dc20   CIP

Published by Focus on the Family Publishing, Colorado Springs, CO 80995
Distributed in the U.S.A. and Canada by Word Books, Dallas, Texas

Scripture quotations are from the Holy Bible, New International Version, Copyright © 1973, 1978, 1984
by the International Bible Society.

Editor: Keith Wall
Cover illustration: David Groff
Art Director: Timothy Jones

Printed in the United States of America

    95 96 97 / 10 9 8 7 6 5

This book is lovingly dedicated to the two most important people in my life:

my husband, Cameron,
and
my daughter, Leah.

Contents

Acknowledgments

Special thanks: To my parents, Jack and Olga Power, for believing in my dreams. Who knows? Maybe this book will hit the best-seller list and we'll buy that boat after all!

To my sister, Helen—confidante, cheerleader and birthing coach extraordinaire! Thanks for lending a hand when I needed it most.

To my family in Christ, the Rileys, for love and support far above the call of duty. With extra special thanks to:

Beth, the world's greatest proofreader.
Amy, for keeping my house clean in spite of me.
Linda, for taking such good care of Leah.

To all the women who have allowed their stories to be told on the pages of this book.

To the wonderful team at Focus on the Family, in order of appearance:

Larry Weeden, for giving me a chance.
Janet Kobobel, for lending her enthusiasm and market savvy to the project.
Keith Wall, for making me look like a better writer than I am.

To my heavenly Father, who has so graciously granted me the desires of my heart.

"Ah, Sovereign Lord, you have made the heavens and the earth
by your great power and outstretched arm. Nothing is too hard
for you."

—Jeremiah 32:17, NIV

Introduction

One of the most common questions people asked me during my pregnancy was, "Are you going to work after the baby arrives?" People were intrigued when I responded that, yes, I was going to work, but I planned to do so from my home. Almost without exception, the women I talked with expressed a strong interest in combining career and family by working at home. Yet they didn't know how to go about making that dream a reality.

I undertook to write this book because I am convinced working at home is a viable option for many women today. As America moves beyond a factory- and office-based economy into the information age, the economic center of society is returning to the home (as it was during the agriculture-based colonial period). Telecommunications equipment, computers and facsimile machines all make working at home an increasingly realistic possibility for millions of Americans. In fact, it is estimated that somewhere between 10 and 25 million Americans already work at home, and the numbers grow larger each day.

At this juncture, the only obstacle to home work is innovation and novelty. People are always resistant to change, even when it's actually a return to a previous way of life. But change must come, and fortunate are those who sense the wave coming in time to ride it.

Will you be one of those who seize the moment?

Part One

So You Want to Work at Home

Balancing Family and Career

I n recent years, a growing number of women have felt torn between the conflicting demands of career and family. Today, financial and societal pressures require the majority of women to return to work before their baby is one year old. Women who opt to stay home often do so at great financial sacrifice. Unfortunately, the tendency has been to present this as an either-or proposition: Either you pursue a career outside of your home or you forgo any opportunity to earn money (and other career benefits) to stay home with your children. However, there *is* another option. You can combine career and family by working at home.

The Impossible Dream?

Many women view working at home as an impossible dream. They conjure up a thousand reasons why it won't work for them: They lack self-discipline, they're not smart enough, they don't know how to get started. It's a lot easier, and much less frightening, to get a safe and secure nine-to-five job. True, there are risks in starting a new home business, however small or large.

But with those risks come opportunities to be your own boss, set your schedule, launch a new career and be accessible to your children.

According to Georgann Fiumara, founder of the 5,000-member Mothers' Home Business Network, "Six years ago, working at home was a strange idea. Now it's commonplace. In a nutshell, home working has become mainstream." People no longer see a home-based business as a last resort or meager sideline. In fact, it has become a very enviable alternative. Ms. Fiumara says the reason some women succeed while others fail is perseverance. "The one who succeeds is willing to do research and educate herself," she said. "She doesn't give up when the least little thing goes wrong."

One Who Dared

Marcia Cone-Esaki is the perfect example of a woman whose perseverance has paid off in a big way. After seven years of working full-time, Marcia decided she had had enough of corporate America. So she turned her love of writing and cooking (along with training in foods and nutrition) into a home-based business. But success didn't come overnight for her and her partner, Thelma Snyder. They struggled for five years, during which time Marcia lived with relatives and often exchanged baby-sitting and household chores for rent.

Things changed dramatically for Marcia when she landed a publishing deal for her third cookbook with a major publisher, Simon and Schuster. To date, *Mastering Microwave Cookery* has sold over 100,000 copies and is entering its fourth year in hardback edition. Altogether, her five cookbooks have sold more than a quarter of a million copies. She has appeared on the "Today" show three times and has been appointed a national spokesperson for The Potato Board and the Campbell Soup Company.

Marcia's articles and recipes have appeared in *Redbook*, *Ladies' Home Journal*, *House Beautiful* and *Working Mother*, just to mention a few. Her work has been praised in publications nationwide, including *People* magazine, *Food & Wine*, the *Chicago Tribune* and the *Baltimore Sun Times*.

The Philadelphia Inquirer heralded *Mastering Microwave Cookery* as the preeminent cookbook for the microwave generation.

Her professional success has enriched her personal life as well. Recently, Marcia's husband, Koji, enrolled full-time in seminary to study for the pastorate. Marcia's income from royalties, speaking fees and a forthcoming book will largely support their entire family of four.

"I can't imagine a better arrangement than what I have," Marcia says. "I am home with my family, but I occasionally get away to travel on business. I use a minimum of child care, and I can move anywhere with my work, depending on my husband's needs. I know this work is a gift from the Lord, and more than once when I thought about giving it up, He has encouraged me to keep going."

Making It Happen

By purchasing this book, you have already taken the first step to establishing your own home business. In the following chapters, you will learn everything you need to know to plan and launch a home business: how to choose a business that is right for you, developing a business plan, time management tips, marketing, cutting through legal red tape, laying a solid financial foundation, and much more.

In addition, an ample section of resources, along with a thorough recommended reading list, is included to help you along the way. You'll also find reproducible forms and charts to help you organize your business and household.

At the end of each chapter, you will find questions to help you clarify pertinent issues and discern the direction of your business. Some chapters also include assignments, enabling you to lay a business foundation in bite-size chunks. I highly recommend that you answer the questions and complete the forms as thoroughly as possible. The more work you do up front, the more likely your business will succeed.

So choose one of the items included on the list of "Hundreds of Things You Can Do From Home" (chapter 17) or invent an idea of your own, and start today to build a better future for yourself and your family.

Questions

1. Why do you want to start a home-based business?

2. What has prevented you from getting started?

3. What do you expect will be the most difficult part?

4. Do you have any possible business ideas right now? If so, list them.

CHAPTER TWO

The Advantages of Homework

L ike any job, working at home offers both advantages and disadvantages. In the days and months ahead, times of discouragement will come. Many women struggle with conflicting priorities and time management. And the physical and emotional demands of promoting your business can be draining. You may begin to wonder if all your hard work is worthwhile, and you may even be tempted to give up your plans. In those moments, turn back to this chapter, reexamine the many benefits of working at home and redouble your efforts to succeed. Remember, anything worth having is worth fighting for.

Be Available for Your Children

The Mothers' Home Business Network recently conducted a survey of home-based businesswomen, and 98 percent of the respondents agreed that homework is the perfect way to juggle the conflicting demands of work and family. Furthermore, 72 percent indicated that being available for their children is the number-one reason they choose to work at home.

According to Donata Glassmeyer, who leads "Mother's Work At Home" workshops, most of the women she meets are interested in homework because day care is undesirable or inadequate, especially for women with more than one child. She explains: "The second child comes along and day care simply becomes too stressful. First one child is sick, and then the other. The cost is too high; caregivers too unreliable."

By working at home, you can avoid the hassles and costs of day care and enjoy spending time with your children. Even if you have to hire a baby-sitter to watch your kids in your home while you work, you will be available in a moment's notice if needed. And you can keep a watchful eye on all that goes on throughout the day, rather than sitting at a desk wondering if your children are okay.

Supplement Your Family's Income

According to the U.S. Bureau of Labor Statistics, most American families in 1990 required a second income to make ends meet. Inflation, health insurance, housing and higher taxes all take a heavy toll on the family income. For some, a home business is ideal, providing flexibility and the opportunity to supplement the family income.

Catherine Smith, proprietor of Cateswear (handcrafted clothing) and single parent of two, has experienced the benefits of earning money *and* being available for her children. "To help our family budget, I had been working two jobs, and it was taking its toll on my kids. Now that I work at home, there's a world of difference in their attitudes, motivation and behavior. They're much more secure just knowing I'm home." Even though it's difficult not having a predictable income, Cate feels the tradeoff is worth it. "When children have only one parent, it's even more important to be available and involved," she says.

Be Your Own Boss

The *Wall Street Journal* recently ran a cover story on "defensive entrepreneurs"—people who, driven by job insecurity, are starting businesses on the side. These people fear dependence on a corporation because they have seen the rug pulled out from under so many of their colleagues. The days when you could rely on a company to look out for your best interests are long gone. While you're working your fingers to the bone for XYZ Corporation, it is entirely possible they are filling out your pink slip.

I experienced this firsthand when I worked in the investment banking department of a large financial institution. Because the corporation had lost nearly half a billion dollars, some three thousand employees had to be laid off. I knew people who had devoted their entire careers — twenty-five or thirty years of their lives — to this corporation. But when the chips were down, they were out on the street, sometimes without even a day's notice.

Eventually, paranoia virtually paralyzed many of my colleagues, and we spent most of the workday worrying about who would be the next to lose his or her job. At times like that, the emotional burden of relying on someone else to sign my paycheck was heavy indeed.

Once you establish your own home-based business, you'll have the pleasure of signing your own paycheck. And when you think you deserve a raise, you can give yourself one.

Set Your Own Hours

Another advantage of being your own boss is setting your own hours. If you want to sleep late, go ahead (as long as you don't do it too often). Want to take four weeks vacation this year? No "Policies and Procedures Manual" will spoil your plans. Do you need to quit early on Wednesdays so your daughter can take ballet lessons? No one will stand in your way.

Jean Haven Amos began her career in real estate almost fifteen years ago. In the beginning, she worked long hours six days a week and, like most new agents, had to take all the in-office floor time she could get, handling phones and helping walk-in clients. Today, she says, "I don't work any floor time. I'm established enough that I don't need it." As a result, Jean only reports to the office when it's absolutely necessary, such as for weekly staff meetings.

Jean feels that real estate offers her tremendous flexibility, and she finds that a substantial amount of her work can be done from home. "A lot of my business involves phone work," she says. "So I can put a load of wash in and then make calls at my kitchen table." Jean has also set up a desk in her bedroom, where she keeps her paperwork. She finds working at home more efficient than the office, because there are fewer interruptions.

Opportunities for Success

When you work nine to five for someone else's company, to a large extent they control how well you do. But when you work for yourself, only your ability and determination set the limits. Maybe there's something you have always dreamed of doing. Now is your chance to do it. You may aspire only to make a little extra money, but there's always the chance that your "silly idea" will catch on and you'll find yourself transformed into a very successful entrepreneur. Someone has to think up those great ideas. Why not you? Maybe you're planning to launch a new full-time career. What an opportunity to start anew!

I was eventually laid off from my job as an investment-banking representative, and it was one of the best things that ever happened to me. It forced me to look at my life and make decisions about what I really wanted to do. As a result, I went back to college to pursue a writing career. If I hadn't lost that job, I wouldn't be where I am today—and you wouldn't be reading this book.

Mental Stimulation

Let's be honest. No matter how much you love being a mother, changing diapers is not exactly on par with performing brain surgery. It's important to develop interests apart from the daily routine or you may find yourself bored and bitter. If you consider "Gilligan's Island" stimulating or find yourself shouting out letters during "Wheel of Fortune," you are very much in need of *constructive* nonmaternal activities. What could be more stimulating and rewarding than running your own business?

Anne Hulley, mother of five and creator of Field Trips Greeting Cards, has found that calligraphing her cards not only provides an outlet for artistic expression, but it also stimulates personal growth. "I try to let the Holy Spirit lead as I design each of my cards," she explains. "The Scriptures I choose are a reflection of my own spiritual growth. This way, I can combine my business, creativity and personal growth."

Anne also appreciates the immediacy of her craft: "Parenting is a matter of faith. You pour yourself into your children and hope your efforts will be rewarded someday. This [the greeting cards] is something from which I can quickly see the fruit of my labor."

Continue Your Career

Many women spend years training for a career before their children arrive on the scene. Teachers, nurses, doctors, lawyers and many other professionals can quite easily transfer their hard-earned skills to a home-based business. Knowing your career is not on hold will give you satisfaction, even though the majority of your time may be spent with family. This is especially important if you want to resume your before-children career.

A Sense of Accomplishment

Believe it or not, God gave the mandate to work *before* the Fall of Mankind (Gen. 2:15). Productive work is not a punishment but an important part of His plan for our lives. Everyone has experienced that exhilarating feeling of working hard to complete a project or the joy of beholding something you've made with your own hands. A home business will provide abundant opportunities for you to enjoy that exhilaration.

In the words of Ellen Lane, a home-schooling mother of three who runs a growing franchise of sewing schools, "I have a real sense of accomplishment knowing I have inspired and motivated others to learn a skill they can benefit from for the rest of their lives." In fact, Ellen is now working with Detroit social workers to teach unwed mothers how to sew. She hopes many of these young women will someday start their own sewing schools — and experience the joy of accomplishment.

Opportunities for Ministry

A number of women start businesses because they see a need and believe they can meet it. That may mean providing services to strengthen individuals or families, or the business itself may be the ministry.

Patricia LeBlanc, founder of Hazen Road QuiltWorks, was motivated by a desire to minister to others. She noticed many of the women at her Mennonite church in rural Vermont made beautiful handcrafted items. She also noticed that they were unable to market them profitably and effectively. So she decided to put her marketing skills to work promoting their quilts, wall hangings and other crafts through a direct mail business. That's how Hazen Road QuiltWorks was born.

Expand Your Sphere of Influence

The most effective way of influencing people for the gospel is by interacting naturally, in the course of our daily lives. As your home-based business gets underway, you will have many opportunities to demonstrate a Christian lifestyle to an ever-widening circle of business associates.

One woman who has influenced many is Alberta Benster, founder of Accessories by Alberta. Over the past eight years, Alberta has provided jobs for fifteen of her neighbors—all working out of their own homes—through her line of children's accessories.

"One of my primary goals in starting this business was to help widows and women with preschoolers," Alberta says. "One of my workers is a widow whose husband died suddenly, leaving her with the care of five children." Alberta finds great satisfaction knowing that she is enabling families to make ends meet. Her business has also provided her with numerous opportunities to develop friendships with her neighbors and share the love of Christ with them in a tangible way.

Questions

1. Which of the advantages discussed in this chapter appeal to you most? Why?

2. Is there something you've always dreamed of doing? How can the dream become a reality through your home-based business?

3. Do you think you will have difficulty being your own boss, setting your own hours, etc? Why or why not?

4. How many hours per week do you plan to work? Write out a tentative work schedule (keep in mind your children's school and nap schedules, etc.).

CHAPTER THREE

Managing Your Time

If you think having four children under age ten would be enough to keep a mother busy, meet Diane Jensen. After her third child began elementary school, Diane found herself growing lazy and bored, even though she still had a four-year-old at home.

Diane started a home-based cleaning service — not because she needed the money, but because she believes in using her time wisely. Diane's motto is "energy breeds energy," which is why you'll find her out for a brisk walk every morning at six. She then gets the kids ready for school, makes breakfast and begins her daily chores. All this is in addition to her twenty-plus hours of cleaning work outside the home.

Diane thinks the secret to her high energy is her ten-minute afternoon nap. She also has a regular weekly schedule she follows religiously. Her well-organized system enables her to earn extra income and still maintain a busy household.

Unfortunately, most women (especially mothers) are not as organized and energetic as Diane. In fact, when I talk with women about starting a home-based business, one of the most frequent objections I hear is, "I couldn't possibly find the time." Yet many women spend thirty or forty hours a week away from home and still manage to keep the household running smoothly. This objection points to an underlying fear that they wouldn't get anything done without a boss hovering over them or a production schedule driving them to meet deadlines.

There's little doubt that your business will fail unless you learn to use your time wisely. Working at home provides many distractions and temptations that could pull you away from your business. How effectively you use your time will largely determine how successful your business becomes.

To help inspire you to use your time wisely, I recommend Charles Hummel's outstanding booklet *The Tyranny of the Urgent* (Downers Grove, Ill.: InterVarsity, 1967). In it, he points out:

> When we stop to evaluate, we realize that our dilemma goes deeper than shortage of time; it is basically the problem of priorities. Hard work does not hurt us. We all know what it is to go full speed for long hours, totally involved in an important task. The resulting weariness is matched by a sense of achievement and joy. Not hard work, but doubt and misgiving produce anxiety as we review a month or year and become oppressed by the pile of unfinished tasks.

Conducting a Time Inventory

I also urge you to conduct a time inventory. This will help you determine how much time you have for a home business and may point out some areas where you can save time. (I have been doing this twice a year since 1981, when I read Michael LeBoeuf's book *Working Smart: How To Accomplish More in Half the Time*, New York, NY: McGraw Hill, 1979.)

Photocopy or re-create the Time Inventory Chart found in chapter 19. Then, for one week, carry the chart with you and jot down how you spend the better part of each half hour (TV, telephone, washing dishes, etc.). But don't suddenly spend two hours in prayer just to make yourself look good. Be honest and try to follow your normal routine as much as possible.

If you're anything like me, this will serve as shock therapy! It may be disconcerting to realize how much of your time is spent on trivial pursuits. Still, the idea is to discern where your time is wasted and strive to recapture it. For me, time flies when I'm on the phone. Like many people, I have a tendency to continue talking long after the usefulness of my words has ceased. If this is an area you struggle with, you may want to keep a close watch on your phone calls as part of your Time Inventory. It might be helpful to set your kitchen clock each time you pick up the phone and, whenever possible, limit your conversation to a predetermined amount of time.

Conquering Time-Wasters

As a self-employed business executive, you can no longer afford to allow time-wasters to control your life. The Bible commands us to "Be very careful, then, how you live — not as unwise but as wise, making the most of every opportunity, because the days are evil" (Eph. 5:15-16). The following tips may help you redeem your time:

■ *Have a daily quiet time*. Ironically, one of the best ways to save time is to spend time. Each morning, set aside a quiet time of Scripture reading, reflection and prayer. This investment will pay rich dividends throughout the day by giving you wisdom to deal with clients and make good decisions.

■ *Learn to say no*. I realize many women, especially Christians, find this difficult. Somehow we have the idea that declining any request for our time and assistance is unspiritual. Nonsense! Jesus did not respond to every request while He walked the earth. In fact, He channeled most of His time and energy into twelve men. Yet He was able to say, "I have brought you glory on earth by completing the work you gave me to do" (John 17:4). As Charles Hummel points out, Jesus was able to do so because "He discerned the Father's will day by day in a life of prayer. By this means He warded off the urgent and accomplished the important" (Hummel, *Tyranny of the Urgent*, 8).

In the same manner, we need to be clear about our calling and purpose. Our top priority, of course, is our walk with the Lord. And for wives and mothers, the second priority must be providing and caring for both the physical and spiritual needs of our families. Be sure to keep first things first. Then if you have time and energy to bake five dozen cookies for the church picnic, terrific. But don't feel you have to comply with every request that comes your way. That's a recipe for disaster.

■ *Don't be a perfectionist*. When good enough is good enough, it's good enough. Is it absolutely necessary to spend seven hours raking the backyard to remove every last leaf when the yard looked okay after an hour? Couldn't the dishes just drip-dry? Do you really have to wipe each one before you put them away? Maybe I sound like a sloppy housewife, but the way I see it, life is too short to waste fussing over minor details.

Remember Parkinson's Law: Work expands to fill the time available for its completion. It even expands to fill time that's *not* available. Especially when it comes to housework, there's always more that could be done. I realize this is a matter of personal preference (and do take your family's viewpoint into consideration), but strive for balance in this area.

■ *Stop procrastinating*. Again, Charles Hummel says it best: "Unanswered letters, unvisited friends, unwritten articles and unread books haunt quiet moments when we stop to evaluate" (Hummel, *Tyranny of the Urgent*, 3). My most exhausting days are the ones in which I've accomplished the least, because frustration and regret saps all my strength.

If a job needs to be done, it's much better to tackle it and get it over with. Then you'll have the satisfaction of crossing it off your To Do list. If your business is going to succeed, you will have to exercise the "spirit . . . of self-discipline" (2 Tim. 1:7). That means pacing yourself to do a little each day, rather than letting things get out of control before you take action.

■ *Stop stewing*. Most would agree that too much of our precious energy is dissipated in bouts of worry, anger and bitterness. Don't allow the difficulties of establishing a business to make you anxious. Worry is a waste of time. Pray about the obstacles you're facing, but don't worry about them (Phil. 4:6-7).

Starting a business requires faith and trust in God's provision, so look at it as an opportunity to grow in these areas. If you find yourself getting discouraged, one of the wisest time investments you can make is memorizing Scripture to counteract negative thought patterns.

■ *Stop shuffling papers.* Paper has a way of invading even the most well-ordered homes. Junk mail, magazines, newspapers, newsletters and the like are insidious time-wasters. Make it a rule to handle each piece of paper that crosses your desk only once, if at all possible. Act on it, clip it, file it or throw it away, but don't spend all your time shuffling around the same old papers.

■ *Tame the telephone and television.* These two monsters can wreak havoc on the best-laid plans. Decide how much time you are willing to spend each day on the two Ts and ruthlessly stick to it. If you have a beautiful twenty-inch color television with a stereo sound system conveniently sitting in the middle of the living room, it's extremely tempting just to flick the switch (especially if you have remote control).

Our small fifteen-year-old black-and-white television is kept in the closet. That way, I have to make a conscious decision to take it out if I want to watch it. Just think, all the time you used to devote to watching game shows can now be channeled into your business endeavors. And which will yield greater rewards?

■ *Schedule shopping trips for off-peak hours and seasons.* Shopping for gifts on Christmas Eve is not very wise, nor is grocery shopping on Saturday afternoon. This is particularly important if your business will involve shopping for supplies often. Also, keep those trips to a minimum by maintaining a list of things you need and buying in bulk.

■ *Make the most of your waiting time.* Rather than reading the tabloid headlines when you're standing in line at the grocery store, pull out your To Do list and bring it up to date, meditate on Scripture passages, pray or jot down any brilliant ideas that come to mind. Do the same while waiting at the dentist office or bus stop. One of the best ways to use waiting time, and to manage your time in general, is by carrying a personal notebook. Remember, your home business will be only as organized as you are.

Your Personal Notebook

Is your house scattered with little slips of paper reminding you of things you're supposed to do or people you have to call? Or worse, is your head cluttered with thoughts like *What was I supposed to do today? What's the deadline for my project? What time does that meeting start?*

You can get rid of your jumbled thoughts and scattered notes by transferring everything into a personal notebook. As a home-based businesswoman, your personal and business lives are intricately intertwined. A notebook will help balance and organize all the competing demands in your life.

Do important birthdays pass by without a call or card from you? Your friends will forgive you, but now that you're a businesswoman, such carelessness may cost you money. That's why the first section of your notebook should be your calendar. Here you will note important events, such as business appointments, deadlines and meetings, as well as things you need to do.

Your notebook should also include an address section. This will come in handy as you seek to develop your business. For example, someone at church may mention that a cousin needs some typing done. You can jot down his name and number in the address section, then turn to your calendar and write "Call Susan's cousin, Bob Smith." Now that you've got it in your notebook, you don't have to worry about forgetting it or misplacing the information. In fact, you don't even have to *think* about it anymore; your notebook will remind you.

Do you end up making several trips to the store to pick up things you forgot to put on your list the first time? Create a Shopping List section. Type up a list of all the things you usually buy each week, along with items that should always be in stock. You will probably want to make one list for food and household goods and another for business-related items. Make photocopies for your notebook. Then simply circle the items you need each week.

Your personal notebook will no doubt include individualized sections. I carry the Day Runner Classic Edition, which includes a month-at-a-glance calendar and special forms for daily schedules, business expenses, and a listing of established and prospective clients. An address book is also incorporated into the notebook. In addition, I've inserted tabs and filler paper for recording goals, prayer requests, sermon notes, Sunday school lessons, books to read and child rearing ideas.

Felice Willat is another woman who believes strongly in the value of carrying a personal notebook. She ought to, since she and her husband founded Day Runner, Inc., one of the most popular personal organizer systems in the world. Day Runner began as a home-based business eleven years ago, starting with a small family savings account and lots of friends and relatives. Today, it has over 350 employees and six million users in twenty countries.

Like so many great ideas, the Day Runner was born out of necessity. Felice was simultaneously working full-time, raising three children and trying to start her own business. She began carrying a three-ring notebook to keep track of opportunities and information as she sought to juggle her multiple roles. Realizing that many people today—especially women—have to manage a wide range of business, social and family activities, Felice and her husband converted her notebook into a marketable product.

The Day Runner product line ranges in price from ten dollars to $275. You can order over the phone by calling **(609) 461-1058**. In addition to the preprinted forms provided, you'll probably want to add customized sections to suit your unique needs. Chapter 18 contains a wide variety of preprinted forms to help you manage your home and business. Simply photocopy those which seem helpful, hole punch and put them to work for you. (I strongly recommend Anne Ortlund's book *The Disciplines of the Beautiful Woman*, which goes into greater detail about setting up and using a notebook.)

Goal Setting

By far, the most important section of any personal notebook should be titled "Goals." I don't mean the resolutions you talk about on New Year's Eve and then forget by January 15. I'm talking about goals that stay with you throughout the year and impact the way you live each day. If you've never set any goals for yourself, now is the time to do so.

Even if it's not January 1 (although that is the ideal time to establish goals), sit down with your notebook, open to the first page of your Goals section and begin to think and pray about what you want to accomplish with your life. These are your *lifetime goals* and may include things like "establish a successful home business employing five other women," "write a book" or "provide college tuition for the kids."

Once you have a good idea of what you want to accomplish in your lifetime, determine what you need to do this year to begin making those goals a reality. These constitute your *yearly goals* and should be more specific. If your lifetime goal is to write a book, your yearly goal may be to write the first five chapters. Or if your lifetime goal is to establish a successful business, this year's goal may be to finish reading this book and decide which business is right for you.

Finally, there are *daily goals*, which are the most specific of all. In other words, if your lifetime goal is to be a godly woman, and your yearly goal is to read through the Bible, you can do so by reading four or five pages per day. Most of the women I know think they could never find time to read the Bible in one year. It seems overwhelming, but don't you think you could read five pages in one day?

If you want to write a book during your lifetime and plan to write five chapters this year, your daily goal may be to write one page per day. That doesn't sound so hard, does it? That's the advantage of breaking down your goals into manageable tasks: things that looked impossible suddenly seem achievable.

It's important to write out your goals and review them frequently (your notebook makes it easy). The Sabbath is a particularly good day to reflect upon the prior week and evaluate how your time and energy were spent in relation to your goals. The Evaluation Worksheet at the end of this chapter will assist you through this process.

A time of reflection will help keep your priorities in focus and ensure that you attend to the important, not just the urgent. Should you desire to make use of the Evaluation Worksheet on a regular basis, a reproducible one is located in chapter 18.

The Fine Art of Delegation

Seventy percent of women surveyed by Ann Landers said they would not raise a family if they could turn back the clock. There are doubtless a variety of reasons why this is so, but I imagine many women are frustrated and exasperated by the incessant work. A lot of mothers feel like slaves to their families, serving as cook, chauffeur, maid and coach all rolled into one. Unfortunately, many women today feel that they alone must do everything involved with running their households and end up wearing themselves out. That is where delegation comes in.

In view of all you do for your children each day, it is not unreasonable to expect them to contribute to the smooth operation of their own household. Don't underestimate their ability to help out around the house. Even small children can and should be taught to clean up after themselves. Yet how many women spend hours each week picking up after Junior? That's not only bad management, it's bad parenting because it produces irresponsible children. Older children can be given responsibilities including meal preparation, dish washing, gardening, etc. That doesn't mean you turn them into a band of slaves and render their lives not worth living. But it does mean instructing children in the lost art of responsibility. Be sure to make good use of the preprinted Chore Charts located in chapter 18.

Mother's Helpers

Even with the assistance of your children, there may be additional household chores that should be delegated so you can devote more time to your business. Proverbs 31:15 says that the wife of noble character provides "portions to her servant girls." Most women zip right by this verse, thinking it's irrelevant to their lives. After all, who could possibly afford to hire servants? But I truly believe the concept of "servant girls" or mother's helpers is an almost universally overlooked resource for today's busy mothers. I propose hiring a junior or senior high school student (a girl is usually best) to serve as your special assistant around the house. She can help out with baby-sitting, cooking, cleaning and errands.

Where can you find such an assistant? First, look to your neighborhood. Perhaps there is a young girl nearby who would be interested in earning some extra money (if not, you're living in a very unusual neighborhood). If you don't have any luck there, try your church youth group or local school.

Let me urge you to view this arrangement as more than just a money-making opportunity for your helper and a convenience for you. Young girls yearn for role models, and what an opportunity for you to model the Christian life! You may have a profound, even eternal, influence on her life as you "speak wisdom" and faithfully instruct her as the Lord leads (see Prov. 31:26). As part of your witness, be sure to give her the "portion" she has earned and encourage her to be a wise steward of her income.

But wait, you may be thinking, *if I have to pay someone to keep an eye on the kids or clean the house, how am I going to make a profit?* If you worked outside your house, you would have to pay someone to watch your children. This arrangement will almost certainly cost you less (I pay between two dollars and five dollars per hour, depending on the job), and you won't have to worry about whether or not your child is receiving good care. And, of course, you'll be immediately available if a problem arises.

For the most part, you will be working side by side as a team. Your helper may be doing the laundry while you work on an article you hope to publish. Or she may play quietly with the children in the backyard while you're on the phone scheduling appointments. I have found this arrangement extremely beneficial. One teenager comes over regularly to help with housecleaning, and a twelve-year-old girl frequently plays with my infant daughter while I work on business projects. If my daughter needs me, or if I just want to take a hug break, she's as close as my living room. And because I'm always close at hand, these girls are not only my employees but special friends as well.

In order to make the principle of delegation work for you, bear in mind two basic guidelines. First, be sure to hire good help. If your next-door neighbor is always complaining about how lazy and difficult her daughter is, she's probably the wrong candidate for the job. Second, your assistant will be only as good as the training and tools you provide. Let your assistant know exactly what is expected, and take the time to teach her. Don't just hand her a bucket of cleaning supplies and go your merry way. That's a formula for misunderstanding and is almost guaranteed to generate ill-will on both sides. Training will be time-consuming at first. You'll probably be frustrated by the realization that you could get the job done quicker (and better) yourself. But investing a little extra time now will save you a great deal more in the future.

As you seek to implement these time-saving strategies, realize that you must find a system that works for you. Some of these tips will work for you; others may not. The important thing is realizing that you really do have enough time to establish and operate your own home-based business.

Questions

I. **Time Inventory***

Once you have completed a week-long Time Inventory in chapter 18, answer the following questions:

1. How and when did I waste time?

2. What activities can be reduced, eliminated or delegated?

3. Did I attend to the truly important, or merely urgent, things in my life?

4. Does my schedule reflect my priorities?

5. Am I using my time to achieve the goals I've set for myself?

6. Whom did I talk to on the phone? Were the calls important and necessary?

7. Did the phone conversations continue beyond necessity? Could they have been shorter and still effective?

* Adapted from Michael LeBouef's *Working Smart: How to Accomplish More in Half the Time.*

II. Weekly Evaluation Worksheet

1. What did I study in my quiet times this week?

2. Which of my business and personal goals did I pursue?

3. Which of my goals did I fail to pursue?

4. Did I attend to the important or merely urgent?

5. Am I using my unique gifts to develop my business?

6. Am I spending time in my office each day?

7. What specific goals do I have for the coming week?

III. General Questions

1.   Indicate below the sections you think you will need for yourpersonal
      notebook.

2.   Make a list of five teenagers you can contact about becoming your
      helper. If you don't know any prospects, contact your church youth
      leader.

Assignments

1.   Buy and set up your own personal notebook.
2.   Hire a helper.

CHAPTER FOUR

Your Children and Your Business

L ynn Lentine didn't discover homework—it discovered her. In 1984, Lynn became pregnant with her first child. She had been working for a small construction company for about five years, but business was slowing down. Since the company's facilities were very primitive, the owner didn't think anyone would want to replace Lynn as the bookkeeper. The boss asked Lynn if she would like to work from her home.

Unfortunately, that arrangement didn't last long. She was laid off after a year and forced to find another job. She took another bookkeeping position for two days a week. Concerned about her son's welfare, Lynn drove two hours and forty minutes every day so she could leave her son with a trusted friend. She knew there had to be a better way to care for her son and keep working.

When a second pregnancy forced her to stay in bed, she offered to do the company payroll from home. It worked out so well that more and more work was sent. This time, the work-at-home arrangement stuck, giving Lynn steady work and the ability to be home with her children.

Today, Lynn provides bookkeeping for two companies. She also works as an at-home supervisor for Christmas Around the World, a home demonstration company. Through this job, Lynn earned a trip to Hawaii for her and her husband, Bob. This year, the entire family is going to Disneyland. That makes it easier for her children, Nick and Alex, to put up with Mommy working!

Lynn's business has grown so much that she can no longer work only at night. She discovered a better way to get things done. Lynn recalls: "It suddenly occurred to me that having a baby-sitter does not necessarily mean Mom is out of the house." So she began hiring teenage girls to occupy the children. That enables her to spend concentrated time working but still be available if needed. Lynn has also learned to work in "snatches" when the kids are napping, in bed for the evening, playing quietly or watching "Sesame Street" (the great reprieve of mothers everywhere).

Lynn believes that operating a home-based business is the best way to be home with young children and still earn money. However, she warns other women not to think it's easier than working outside the home. "In some ways, it's harder because you're always at the office, yet family and others expect you to be a full-time homemaker," she says. "The key is to realize you are a working mother, even though you don't walk out the door at eight o'clock each morning. Even though it's tough sometimes, I feel like it's the best solution. I'm available for my kids, but I still have the challenge and income that work provides."

Children Benefit When Mom Works at Home

Like Lynn, many work-at-home mothers are realizing the benefits for themselves and their children. The opportunity to spend time with their kids during the preschool years is of prime importance to an increasing number of women. School-age children benefit from having a mother at home as well.

Author Betty Beach surveyed parents about their reasons for wanting to work at home. Beach said: "Interestingly, most parents expressed that their motivation for working at home was to be available to very young children;

however, it appears from children's interviews and observations that parental access remains crucial to the relationship long after the preschool years" (*Integrating Work and Family Life*, New York, NY: The State University of New York Press, 1989, 135). Both elementary and high school students were very enthusiastic about having a parent home when they returned from school each day, even if it meant having only a few minutes to recap the day's events. Children derive tremendous security just knowing a parent is available.

Still, some obstacles must be overcome if a mother is going to succeed in a home business. Chief among those obstacles is keeping your children busy so you can get some work done.

Occupying Your Children

One advantage children of working mothers have over those of stay-at-home moms is a greater sense of independence and creativity. When a child only has to say "Mom, I'm bored" (as they so frequently do) and Mom comes running with a book full of games and activities, he really doesn't need to draw upon his own resources very often. When *Mom* is bored (dare I say it?), she ends up picking up his toys, cleaning his room and taking care of his chores. As a result, the child may learn to be dependent and irresponsible.

A working mother simply doesn't have time to do these things. And if she's smart, she sees to it that the child takes full responsibility. Believe it or not, I actually remember being jealous of one of my grade-school classmates because her parents were divorced and she lived with her working mother. When she got home each day, she found a note from her mother listing chore assignments. As she finished each item, she crossed it off her list. In return, she received an allowance with which to buy clothes or, best of all, go roller-skating.

It seemed like my life was so dull in comparison. I got home and watched TV while Mom cooked. When I wanted money for roller-skating or clothes, I begged, pouted and generally acted like a brat until Mom gave in. I now realize the heartache of children from broken homes, but I still admire the sense of responsibility instilled in my childhood friend.

The children of home working mothers can have the best of both worlds—an available mom and a strong sense of responsibility. The following are just a few suggestions for balancing the demands of your children and your business. Depending upon the age and temperament of your children, some of the ideas will work; others may not. Experiment with several options, invent your own and find out how other homeworking mothers cope.

■ *Office hours.* It is wise to set aside a specific time each day to work. During that time, post a "Mom Working" sign and instruct the children to play quietly, read, draw or color. You might let the kids have their own office space, where they can work while you do. Give them paper, crayons, scissors, or if possible, scrap material related to your business, and let them have their own projects just like Mom.

Be sure to establish a tradition of coffee breaks so the kids can look forward to a special time with you. They'll be less likely to interrupt if they know that at 10:30, Mom *always* spends a half hour with them.

■ *Chore chart.* Developing a chore chart is advisable for all mothers but *mandatory* for homeworking mothers. The children can be encouraged to work on their chores during your office hours. In addition to household duties, they may also be assigned jobs related to your business. (See Dr. James Dobson's book *Dare to Discipline* for further details on assigning chores.)

■ *Sibling care.* If you have both preschool and school-age children, the older children can entertain the younger ones for a period of time each day. You might reward them with a special treat or extra allowance for helping in this way.

■ *Friends and relatives.* If you have friends or relatives nearby, particularly with children close in age to your own, they may be willing to help out from time to time. Your mother, sister or next-door neighbor may agree to watch your children, especially if you can get them excited about your business (offer to keep them in mind when you hit the big time).

In addition to helping me out with free child care, my sister, Helen, is my number-one cheerleader and a great sounding board for ideas. In return, I help her with her nursing school assignments.

■ *Neighborhood or church play groups.* Join other mothers with children close in age to yours to form a play group. Then one day a week (or whatever is agreeable), have all the children gather at one of the homes on a rotational basis. Depending upon the size of the group, your turn to supervise may come once a week or once a month.

■ *Television.* Of course, TV should never be used as a baby-sitter, but once in a while *quality* television is okay. Perhaps you can let your youngsters watch "Sesame Street" each morning while you work. The Disney Channel and Nickelodeon also offer some excellent programs. If you own a VCR, you can even buy or rent Christian videos, such as the *McGee & Me* series available from Focus on the Family.

■ *Hire a mother's helper.* Mother's helpers were discussed in chapter 3. Basically, this involves hiring and training a teenage girl to work at your home, occupying your children while you work or helping out with household chores. If your business becomes extremely successful, you can even hire a full-time nanny. Why not think big?

■ *Preschool.* You may want to consider enrolling your child in a reputable preschool a couple of mornings per week. Many churches are now offering excellent programs. This will not only provide you with work time, it will offer your children opportunities for socialization and help prepare them for kindergarten.

Employing Your Children

As your children watch you carry out the daily tasks of your business, they will come to respect you as a businessperson and as someone whose whole world does not revolve solely around them. Believe it or not, being the center of their parents' world is a heavy load for children to carry. They *want* Mom to have a life of her own.

The previously cited study conducted by Betty Beach revealed that children of home-based workers were very familiar with the everyday affairs of their parent's business (unlike the average kid, who may only know that Dad works in an office). They were far more informed about the nature of their parent's work than were other children, and most of those interviewed were able to describe actual tasks their parent performed and the tools required.

Beach discovered that children were aware of and involved with the conduct of business in "progressively age-appropriate ways." The four levels of progressive involvement are: play-watch-help; simple tasks; assistance with work on a regular basis; and regular, paid work. (For more information, see Betty Beach's *Integrating Work and Family Life*, Albany, NY: State University of New York Press, 1989.)

■ *Play-watch-help.* Even very young children demonstrate a keen interest in the activities of their working parents. These youngsters enjoy interrupting their play to observe or help out. At this stage, the child's involvement is strictly spontaneous (e.g., a three-year-old might come over and ask if he or she can hold mommy's spool of yarn but will not do so on a consistent or long-term basis).

My daughter, Leah, loves to sit on my lap while I work on the computer and likes to tap-tap-tap the keyboard. I have a playpen in my office that I place her in only when I really need to concentrate.

■ *Simple tasks.* Young children can be taught to perform simple tasks, such as stuffing envelopes or sorting colored papers. At this stage, helping out should be more fun than work.

Donna Kessel, president of Lynne Designs, allows her two-year-old to open all mail received for her mail-order business. Catherine Smith, proprietor of Cateswear, reports that "work has become a family affair. Two-year-old Kyle is the chief scrap collector and Kris, thirteen, answers the phones and packs orders."

■ *Assistance with work on a regular basis, paid or unpaid.* As children get older, they can be assigned regular business-related tasks, just as they would be given other household chores. Whether or not you pay your children is a personal decision. Some mothers want to teach their children that everyone should make a contribution to the family, while others feel payment is both a reward and preparation for money management.

Ellen Lane, who runs a sewing school, has incorporated business-related chores into her children's home-school curriculum. In addition, she pays her two oldest children, ages eight and ten, to sweep up material scraps after classes.

Patricia LeBlanc, founder of Hazen Road QuiltWorks, hires her three sons, ages nine, eleven and fifteen, to package her quilts for mailing. She also pays them to stuff brochures into envelopes. Her three-year-old daughter, Bethany, is also certain to join the QuiltWorks payroll someday. Even at her young age, she is already in charge of removing the safety pins from Mom's finished quilts.

■ *Regular, paid work.* Rather than flipping burgers at McDonald's, your teenager can learn your trade and earn money while preparing for the future. Jean Haven Amos, a real estate agent, hires her teenage daughter, Amy Jo, to distribute a monthly bulletin to houses throughout her territory. Not only is Amy Jo earning money and learning about real estate, she has also learned what it's like to be an employer. To make the work go faster—and to have more fun—Amy Jo frequently hires friends to help with the flyer distribution. Her mother pays her a set amount per bulletin, and Amy Jo in turn pays her "employees."

Training Them for the Future

Having participated in your business, your children will have a greater knowledge of the business world. They'll also be able to avoid the "Catch 22" most young people face when they're first starting out: You can't get a job without experience, and you can't get experience without a job.

By assisting you with your business, your children will also learn the value of a dollar, and they will better appreciate when their needs are provided— not by some mysterious paycheck but as a direct result of money they've watched you earn by the sweat of your brow. In the words of Linda Cox, who makes stuffed animals, "I think it's good that my work is so visible to my children (ages seven and eleven). They understand the relationship between work and home, and they see where the money comes from to pay our bills. Family finances are more realistic to them now."

If your business becomes successful, or particularly enjoyable to your children, you may even pass it along to them as an inheritance.

Questions

1. Which of the techniques for occupying your children do you plan to implement? How and when will you do so?

2. How can you involve your children in your business? Will they serve as occasional helpers or do you intend for them to become regular employees?

CHAPTER FIVE

Keys to Success

I f you've read this far, you are probably quite determined to launch a career as a home-based businesswoman. The perks and benefits sound great — naming your own hours, generating income, being accessible to your children. Still, fear and self-doubt may be holding you back. *I don't have the business smarts*, you may think. *Besides, I have no special abilities or training. How can I go into business for myself? What if I fail?* I assure you, such feelings are quite normal and can be overcome.

You do not need a Harvard Business School degree or an MBA to prosper as an entrepreneur. As a mother, you have accumulated far more skills and abilities than you give yourself credit for. You must rid yourself of the notion that a successful business must be something terribly complex and difficult. Some of the most prosperous businesses are the most simple. And besides, success, like anything else, is in the eye of the beholder.

For you, success may be contributing a few extra dollars to the family budget — or it may be building a full-fledged career. Set your own goals, and when you achieve them, consider yourself a success. But whether you want to establish a Fortune-500 company or just earn an extra fifty dollars a week, there are a few key ingredients that will help you reach your goals. We'll examine nine elements that will enable you to build a successful business.

Choose a Business You Really Enjoy

Time and time again, home businesses fail because the proprietor selected an endeavor for all the wrong reasons: *The woman down the street is starting a typing service and I can, too*. Never mind that you *hate* to type, there's money to be made and you intend to make it. That, my friend, is a formula for disaster.

Choose a business you can pour your heart into, something you can believe in and feel good about. Consider your talents, interests and background, and strive to match these to your new venture. You'll enjoy your business more and will be less prone to burn out.

Conduct Thorough Research Before You Begin

Almost all the successful women I interviewed have taken courses on some aspect of running a small business. They have also taken advantage of the free counseling and training services available to them through the Small Business Administration, local university extension services and similar nonprofit organizations.

Don't be a stranger to the library, either. Read up on your line of business and find out how other people in similar circumstances have succeeded. Also, be sure to learn what competition exists in your area. The more research you do *before* opening your doors for business, the longer those doors will stay open. (Chapter 19 is filled with information on helpful resources. Be sure to take advantage of all the help available to you.)

Be Persistent

Your business is not going to succeed overnight. However, if you believe your endeavor is worthwhile and you really want to work from home, all that remains is planning and persistence. In time, you will reap the harvest, but first you must plant the seeds! Don't be content with the current "crop" of clients or your business will soon dry up.

Be willing to invest the time and energy required to continually cultivate future business. Send out flyers to people who have never used your product or service before, and send thank you notes to those who have. Maintain a list of previous customers and mail them a newsletter or updated product list from time to time, just to keep your name fresh in their minds.

Persistence plays a particularly important role in getting started. You may run into obstacles and resistance, and you may be tempted to give up. Knocking on doors and drumming up business day after day can be emotionally and physically tiring. The difference between those who fail and those who succeed often comes down to knocking on one more door.

Discipline Yourself

There's no doubt that self-discipline is critical for success. To some it comes naturally, while others have to work at it. Of course, the degree of self-discipline required varies according to circumstances. A mother of five who works forty hours a week requires more self-discipline than an empty-nester working twenty hours.

If this is an area you struggle with, *don't let that hold you back*. Go straight out and buy Anne Ortlund's *Disciplines of the Beautiful Woman*. Self-discipline, more than any other characteristic included here, can be learned. Establish accountability with your spouse, partner or friend, and determine deadlines and checkpoints for progress.

Work Like a Professional

Your image is an extremely important part of your business. Although it's hard to define precisely what is meant by "professional," there are a number of factors that can work together to ensure you make a favorable impression on your associates and clients.

■ *Your appearance*. It's nice that home-based businesswomen don't have to spend a fortune on clothing and grooming supplies. What you wear while working around the house is no one's business but your own. In fact, you can skip the morning makeup madness altogether if you wish. On the other hand, if you want to set an atmosphere to promote work, you may find that wearing a professional-looking outfit is more inspiring than your old bathrobe and fuzzy slippers. On those occasions when you do come in contact with the public, be sure to present the image appropriate to your industry and clientele.

■ *Your office.* If clients or vendors come to your home, your office should be neat, professional and clearly distinguished from the rest of the house (see chapter 8). If your office can be reached only by passing through the rest of the house, be sure it's clean and orderly before potential clients see it. As much as possible, try to be available during normal business hours.

■ *Phone manners.* Much of your business will probably be conducted over the phone, so make sure you or another responsible adult answers the phone in a professional manner. If your children often use your residence line, it is wise to install a separate business phone unless you can prohibit them from answering the family phone (good luck!). An answering machine is also a wise investment, enabling you to receive calls when you are away from home. Even if you are home but madness is reigning, it's better to let the machine take the call. You can respond once the household is under control again.

Build a Solid Support System

Over and over again, the women interviewed for this book said one of the keys to their success was a supportive husband, family and friends. Unfortunately, this is something you have little control over—but you can exert some influence. Long before you put up the "Open for Business" sign, work to win the enthusiastic support of your family and friends. Sell them on your ideas and assure them you are serious about your endeavor.

Once things are underway, you can head off potential conflicts by clarifying expectations. Prior to going into business, you may have taken your child's forgotten book to school or dropped off a report at your husband's office. Make it clear that you remain willing to help in a crisis, but by and large your family shouldn't expect you to do all the things you once did as a full-time housewife. (Balance this with grace and mercy, of course!)

If you are moving from full-time outside employment to a home-based business, make sure your family understands that you're still *working*—just in a different place. In other words, if you worked at a downtown office from nine to five, would your daughter expect you to drop everything to bring lunch money to school? Of course not. Be very careful here or you can end up with the *worst* of both worlds: the pressures of a working mother and none of the slack usually afforded.

Friends also may have expectations you will no longer be able to fulfill. Perhaps you used to make five dozen brownies from scratch for PTA meetings. Let them know they'll have to settle for store-bought cookies or find another refreshment volunteer. Maybe a special friend is in the habit of dropping in unannounced during the day. She needs to know you're unavailable for socializing during work hours. All of this should be done with tact, of course, so feelings aren't hurt and friendships aren't damaged.

On the positive side, you can enlist the aid of your friends. One of my best friends, Beth Riley, serves as my proofreader. This project has drawn us closer and has built mutual respect. Alberta Benster, founder of Accessories by Alberta, which makes children's hair and clothing accessories, has provided jobs for fifteen of her neighbors and friends.

Cultivate Self-Confidence

When you exude confidence in your skills and services, your customers and clients will be reassured as well. Likewise, if you're unsure about what you have to offer, others are likely to detect this and have the same misgivings.

One way to gain confidence is to do your homework and be fully prepared. Be precise and knowledgeable about every aspect of your business. Know your products, customers and competition. You can't afford to wing it. Have your spouse or a friend ask you tough questions about your venture. Also, completing the forms at the back of this book and answering the questions at the end of each chapter will help instill confidence, forcing you to think through all the details of launching your business.

You certainly don't need to apologize for being a home-based business woman. What you're doing is extremely important. Think of yourself as an exciting trend setter, paving the way for future generations of mothers.

Learn to Deal Effectively With Others

Your business will inevitably bring you into contact with many new people, including customers, subcontractors and vendors. Your ability to deal effectively with them will directly affect your success.

Each morning, you should pray over the day's events, the people you are scheduled to meet and the unexpected interruptions that will occur. Ask God to give you wisdom and grace as you deal with each one.

Be Flexible

Days will come when your son or daughter has a 104-degree temperature. Or perhaps it's sunny and eighty degrees and simply too beautiful *not* to go to the park. As long as you do not behave irresponsibly (e.g., missing a deadline), you can scrap the daily schedule every now and then. You're the boss, so give yourself a day off once in a while.

Flexibility, however, is also necessary to meet the challenges of combining career and family. You may have to postpone a meeting to take your child to the hospital, or you may be forced to bail out of a family outing to meet a pressing deadline. It's all part of being a home-based entrepreneur!

Do You Have What It Takes?

Not every home business is a smashing success. In fact, some are doomed to failure before they begin. The following evaluation tool will help determine if you're prepared to launch your business.

Home-based Business Success
Evaluation Tool

Rate yourself on a scale of one to ten, with ten being the highest.

Quality	Rating
You are persistent when the going gets tough	_____
You are self-disciplined (no boss is watching you)	_____
You are professional (you *are* your business)	_____
You are imaginative (able to go from idea to product)	_____
You are courageous and willing to take calculated risks	_____
You are patient (it takes time to lay a solid foundation)	_____
You are a planner (able to plan ahead)	_____
You are self-confident (to carry out your plans)	_____
You are resilient (able to bounce back from disappointments)	_____
You have selected a business you enjoy	_____
You have thoroughly researched your endeavor	_____
You have developed a support system to encourage you	_____
You have acquired faith to cope with financial insecurity	_____
You have a sense of humor	_____
Total	_____

Rating Scale

101 +	What are you waiting for? Go for it!
76 - 100	Consider yourself most likely to succeed.
51 - 75	Likely to succeed.
26 - 50	Give it your best shot.
0 - 25	It's probably not for you.

Part Two

ESSENTIAL DETAILS OF A HOME-BASED BUSINESS

CHAPTER SIX

Laying a Solid Business Foundation

Establishing any business requires both time and money. Before taking another step forward, sit down and honestly evaluate how much of each you are willing and able to invest. This will determine, in large measure, the nature of the business you should undertake.

If you are unwilling to borrow thousands of dollars and risk your home as collateral, don't attempt to launch a nationwide clothing franchise. If you have five children and can't possibly devote twelve hours a day, six days a week, you probably shouldn't open a full-scale catering service. Like anything else in life, it is a matter of trade-offs.

Remember the old saying "nothing ventured, nothing gained"? You will get out of your business whatever you're willing to put into it. No more and no less. Do you envision yourself as a world-renowned entrepreneur? Wonderful. Be prepared to pay the price. On the other hand, maybe you simply need to earn a hundred dollars per week to supplement the family income. That's great, even though you'll never be among the rich and famous. The important thing is to be clear about your priorities.

What Business Is Right for You?

By far the most important decision you have to make is what type of business to launch. Remember, this is a very personal matter, and what's right for someone else isn't necessarily right for you. Don't make the mistake of leaping into an arena that may be totally unsuitable for you just because opportunities exist.

Donna Kessel, founder of Lynne Designs, Inc., started *three* home-based businesses before finding one she enjoyed. All three failed, because she went into them for the wrong reasons. "I made decisions based on what was convenient and what I had the equipment to do," she says. "I saw other women making money and figured I could do it the same way."

Today, Donna runs a successful mail-order business manufacturing and selling baby bracelets. She has one employee (who works out of her own home) and earns a very respectable salary working just twenty-five hours per week. Donna strongly urges other women to choose a business they really enjoy: "Do something you've always wanted to do, something you can put your heart into. Don't choose something just to make money."

That's about the best advice anyone can give you. So set aside some time to complete the Skills and Interests Inventory at the end of this chapter. Since being objective about yourself may be difficult, ask your spouse or a friend to complete the Third-Party Analysis Worksheet. By comparing the two evaluations, you will get a good idea of your strengths.

Developing a Business Plan

You've probably heard the saying "Failing to plan is planning to fail." Nowhere is this more true than business. Once you have determined what business is right for you, the next step is writing a business plan. Don't make the mistake of relying on intuition or vague, unwritten objectives. Get your plan in writing.

An important part of being taken seriously is taking yourself and your business seriously. So be sure to take the extra time to produce a plan that is thorough, accurate and neat. If you plan to remain a one-woman operation forever, it need not be more than a couple of pages. Nevertheless, it's a vital document that indicates to you and all interested parties (financial institutions, insurance agencies, etc.) where you plan to go and how you intend to get there. To help you get started, I've included a Business Plan Worksheet later in this chapter.

Before you set about devising your business plan, take a few minutes to answer the following ten questions. They will help guide you through the planning process.

1. What do you enjoy doing with your free time? If you enjoy horseback riding, why not become an instructor?

2. Are any of your hobbies or talents marketable? If you're good enough to play piano at church, surely you would be able to offer at least beginner-level lessons. Do you like to cross-stitch? Why not sell some of your projects?

3. Are you imaginative and inventive? How about writing greeting cards? Or are you more detail-oriented and enjoy repetition? In that case, you could serve as a bookkeeper for a local doctor.

4. Do you possess any technical skills? Maybe you worked as a systems analyst before the children were born; why not start a computer consulting business?

5. What do other people say you're good at? What do *you* think you're good at? If everyone raves about your cooking, consider starting a catering business. Offer cooking lessons in your own kitchen. Have you come up with desert recipes you know are terrific? Why not bake them and offer them exclusively through a local, upscale restaurant? *Forbes* magazine recently profiled Debbi Fields, founder of Mrs. Fields, Inc. People liked her chocolate chip cookies so much she went into business at the age of 20. That was in 1977; today her holdings are worth $63 million ("Succeeding By Failing" by Katherine Weisman, *Forbes*, June 25, 1990). Maybe you've got a million-dollar recipe on your hands. You'll never know unless you try.

6. What type of support will be available to you? If you will be working on your own, a modest business venture with minimal investment is best. Perhaps you could do housecleaning two mornings a week. If, on the other hand, you've got a supportive husband and two teenage kids looking to earn extra money, perhaps you can launch an office-services company and get the whole family involved.

7. How much time are you able to devote to your home-based business? A mother with two preschoolers has a lot less free time available than a woman with an empty nest. The first may want to plan children's parties on an occasional basis, whereas the empty-nester will want steadier work, such as a mail-order business.

8. How much money do you want or need to earn? If the family budget is coming up four hundred dollars short per month, five haircuts a week (twenty dollars each) will cover it. But if you've made major financial commitments based on two incomes and a baby has just arrived, you had better aim higher.

9. What are some problems you've solved as a mother? What are some gadgets you've come up with to make life easier? Chances are, other mothers are facing similar dilemmas. Think of the person who came up with the "Baby on Board" sign a few years back. How many times did *you* think to yourself, *I wish people realized I'm driving slowly because the baby is in the car*. A recent craze was glare screens for car windows. Hasn't every mother tried her own techniques for keeping the sun out of her baby's eyes? Someone has to invent these gadgets. Why not you? If you've got an innovative solution to a common problem, why not develop it into a marketable product?

10. Finally, list all the activities you usually do in an ordinary week (grocery shopping, cooking, etc.). Then analyze each area to determine what skills are involved (writing, planning, communication, etc.). What personal qualities (flexibility, self-motivation) enable you to accomplish these tasks successfully? Now, how can you channel those skills and personal qualities into a business venture?

Skills and Interests Inventory

1. List five things you enjoy doing with your free time.

2. List any hobbies or talents you have that may be marketable.

3. What type of temperament do you have: creative or analytical? meticulous or carefree? determined or easily discouraged?

4. List any technical or unique skills you possess.

5. List five things other people say you're good at.

6. List five things you think you're good at.

7. What type of support will be available to you?

8. How much money do you want or need to earn?

   Per week _____ Per month _____ Per year _____

9. What are some problems you've solved as a mother? Have you designed some gadgets to make life easier?

10. List all the activities you usually do in an ordinary week in the "Task" column, and indicate the skills involved in the "Skills" column.

   Task   **Skills Involved**

   _____   _____
   _____   _____
   _____   _____
   _____   _____
   _____   _____
   _____   _____
   _____   _____
   _____   _____
   _____   _____
   _____   _____

11. Based on this information, list ten possible home-based businesses that might be suitable for you (refer to the list in chapter 17 for inspiration, if necessary).

Third-Party Analysis

Complete the following exercise, evaluating the skills and interests of your friend or spouse. The information will be most helpful if you are as honest as possible.

1. List five things she seems to enjoy doing with her free time.

2. List any hobbies or talents she has that may be marketable.

3. What type of temperament does she have: creative or analytical? meticulous or carefree? determined or easily discouraged?

4. List any technical or unique skills she possesses.

5. List five things other people say she is good at.

6. How supportive of a business venture will her friends and family be?

7. How much time do you think she could devote to a home-based business?

    Per day _____ Per week _____

8. Based on the above, list five possible home-based businesses that might be suitable.

Business Plan Worksheet

As you continue reading this book, the answers to each of these questions will emerge, so consider your Business Plan a document-in-progress at this point. For now, leave blank any questions you aren't sure about. You should turn here again and again as you move closer to starting a home-based business.

1. Describe the business in detail:

    Company Name: _____

    Address: _____

    _____

    Owner: _____

    Legal Structure: _____

    (Attach copies of legal documents to your business plan.)

2. State the major goals and objectives of the business:

    _____

    _____

    _____

3. Discuss the special skills and experiences you bring to the company. Describe your qualifications. (Attach a resume to your business plan.)

    _____

    _____

    _____

4. Describe the products or services offered.

    _____

    _____

    _____

5. What advantages do your products or services have over those already on the market?

    _____

    _____

    _____

6. Describe your market (those people most likely to buy your product or service).

    _____

    _____

    _____

    _____

7. List current customers, if any.

    _____   _____

    _____   _____

    _____   _____

8. Indicate when, where and how you plan to advertise and publicize your business.

    _____   _____

    _____   _____

    _____   _____

    _____   _____

9. List all equipment and supplies you will require to get started.

    _____   _____

    _____   _____

    _____   _____

    _____   _____

10. Indicate how much money you will need to start. Beside these figures, project how you will obtain it. (Attach a copy of your start-up and first-year budgets.)

Amount   **Funding Source**

_____   _____

_____   _____

_____   _____

_____   _____

_____   _____

_____   _____

_____   _____

_____   _____

_____   _____

CHAPTER SEVEN

Marketing

Posy Lough, co-founder of The Posy Collection, did her homework before launching her business. Since 1977, Posy has successfully sold Christmas ornaments, handcraft cross-stitch kits, notecards, booklets and other specialty items.

According to Posy, the secret of her business success is carefully targeting a specific market. She developed products for sale in gift shops in Monticello, Mount Vernon and Epcot Center. She knew the types of customers these stores catered to, and she targeted them directly. Later, Posy contacted *Focus on the Family* magazine, which ran a brief article on her line of Christian products. The result was thousands of orders and the turning point in Posy's business.

Posy wisely researched who exactly would be interested in buying her products—and then figured out how to present the products to potential customers. To be successful, you must do the same.

First of all, you must identify your "market." In other words, you need to determine which individuals or organizations will want or need your product or service. If your business is making baby bracelets, the people most likely to buy your product are new parents. *The Encyclopedia of Associations* provides customer profiles and industry data by subject and will give you an excellent idea of people who will be interested in your product or service.

This is perhaps the most important step in establishing your business. You may be able to make terrific nose warmers, but if you try to sell them to Hawaiians in July, you're not going to get very far. In order to evaluate the viability of your idea, answer the questions presented at the end of this chapter. You may want to answer them separately for each business you are considering. This process will help you decide which of your ideas are most likely to succeed.

Once you've determined which proposed business is most feasible, you need to develop an effective marketing strategy. Your home-based business will succeed or fail depending upon how carefully you develop a marketing plan. You may offer the greatest service in the history of the world, but if no one has ever heard of your product or service, you won't be in business very long.

Marketing Strategies

Marketing may sound like a complex subject, but actually it's quite simple. Any communication between you and a potential customer is marketing. That includes everything from paid advertisements in newspapers to your business cards. When you send out a letter, the aesthetic impression it makes (quality of the stationery, neatness and accuracy) is just as important as the actual content. Your company name and logo also communicate volumes, so choose them carefully. The way you answer the telephone and greet people in person also says a great deal about the business you run.

Different industries require different approaches. What will work for a quilt-maker will not work for a secretarial service. I recommend you consult a book specifically geared to marketing in your field (see chapter 20 for a recommended reading list). But, in general, marketing strategies can be divided into three categories: advertising, public relations and networking.

Advertising

The key to successful paid advertising (and marketing in general) is to keep in mind the four Rs: Marketing must be done at the *right time*, at the *right price*, and be presented in the *right way* to the *right people*. That's why knowing your market is so important *before* you invest any money. If you are making a country decor product, advertising in *Time* magazine is not a wise choice, but *Country Home* magazine definitely is. Christmas stockings probably won't do very well in June, but advertise the same product in the same place in November, and see what a difference timing makes. Today, a multitude of media exist through which you can reach out to potential customers:

■ *Newspapers*. If your product is general enough to attract a wide audience, advertising in newspapers is a relatively inexpensive way to reach a large number of people in your local area. Newspapers offer both display and classified advertising space. Try to place your advertisement in the section that the most likely buyer is most likely to be reading. For instance, if you are offering cooking classes, place a display ad in the foods section.

■ *Magazines*. Today, magazines are highly specialized. There are magazines for working moms, sports fans, businessmen, exercise buffs and couch potatoes. Magazine advertising space is more expensive than newspapers, but you can better target the market you want to reach. As a result, the return on your investment may be much greater. Spend some time at a nearby magazine rack or library. Which magazines would be of interest to people who might buy your product? Contact the magazine by letter or telephone and ask them to send you demographics (statistics on who reads their magazines) along with pricing information. This will help you determine where to invest your advertising dollars.

■ *Radio and television*. Advertising on radio and TV can be very expensive. But it can also be very profitable. Although not recommended for the home-based businesswoman on a tight budget, if you have solid cash flow and have thoroughly investigated the potential return on your investment, you may be ready for this step. If so, consult a professional advertising agency for assistance in developing an ad campaign.

■ *Direct mail*. You probably don't like receiving junk mail, but sending it may prove very profitable for you. This is an effective way of marketing certain types of products. For instance, you wouldn't buy a car through the mail, but you might respond to a limited-time offer to join a book club for your children—especially when you get the first five books for a penny.

Within a week after I brought my baby home from the hospital, the deluge of mail solicitations began. Everyone knew that Mrs. Partow had a new baby. Wouldn't I like portraits taken? How about a personalized bracelet, mug, bib or diaper bag? Was I interested in receiving a toy once a month? Would I like to join a book club for the baby? You get the picture! And yes, as a new mother, I *was* interested in some of these things. Where did these people get my name? They bought a mailing list of new mothers.

Direct mail firms across the country offer mailing lists for every category you can imagine. For a price, you can receive a list of everyone who bought a new house within the last few months (so you can try to sell them welcome mats). Again, the key is knowing your market.

Donna Kessel, founder of Lynne Designs, discovered the advantages of direct mail. For a number of years, Donna sold her baby bracelets through retail stores. Although she was successful, that approach involved a lot of running around. Today she pays a fee to a direct mail firm that provides gift packs to new mothers. In return, they place her brochure in the pack, which is distributed to three million new mothers nationwide.

■ *Yellow Pages.* Once you install a separate business telephone line, you are entitled to a listing in the Yellow Pages under the heading of your choice. You are also allowed to purchase a display ad for a modest price. Many entrepreneurs believe a display ad in the yellow pages is the best advertising investment they ever made.

■ *Flyers.* It's Saturday afternoon. Time to go shopping. As you walk through the mall, a young girl hands you a five-by-eight-inch piece of paper. Macy's is having a shoe sale. You come out of the mall and return to your car, only to find that a flyer is lodged under your windshield wiper. You're probably annoyed, but curiosity wins out and you glance at it. You arrive home and a flyer is rolled up in the door handle. Do you read it on the way to the trash can?

The great thing about flyers is the price. You can write your own and have it photocopied for a modest fee. On the down side, you'll probably have to distribute thousands of them to get any result. But again, keep in mind the four Rs. If you're opening a secretarial service, you may want to visit a nearby college campus to pass out flyers. But handing them out at the grocery store probably wouldn't make sense.

■ *Word of mouth*. The best form of advertising in the world is word of mouth, and the only way to get it is to earn it. Treat your customers right. Provide them with top-notch service or merchandise in a timely and courteous fashion, and the customers will come to you.

Public Relations

Simply said, public relations is anything that gets your name before the public. This may involve providing services or products in return for goodwill, and hopefully, future business. When you donate ten dozen cookies to the local fair, carefully wrapped and clearly labeled "Sharon's Cookies," that's good public relations. Everyone thinks you're an incredibly nice person for giving away free cookies—and if they like them, they may become paying customers.

If you own a furniture rental business, you could lend several pieces for a local college theater production in exchange for a mention in the program. Or you may help sponsor a free blood-pressure screening at the local mall. In return, your business name might be included in promotional ads or posters.

An important component of public relations is publicity. This is exposure provided by the media, free of charge. Understand that publicity is only granted when it's in the media's best interest, not yours. The *New York Times* is not going to write a story about you so you can sell more of your homemade Teenage Mutant Ninja Turtle dolls. But they might run the story as part of an examination of current trends in youth culture. Remember that there are many different sides to any story (mothers know all about that, right?). Be sure to slant yours accordingly.

When you seek publicity, present your story in terms that will interest the newspaper or magazine's editorial staff. Is your product truly intriguing or unique? Is it designed to meet an emerging need? Does it reveal something about your community or the country at large? For example, my sister-in-law lives in a community that, until very recently, was predominantly Amish. She is offering a catering service, which is obviously not of interest to the Amish. However, the community has been deluged with Yuppies over the past two to three years. A catering service is not interesting news; the fact that Yuppies are flocking to the country is. The first angle would not yield publicity; the second very well might.

Carefully examine newspapers and magazines in which you would like to obtain coverage. Determine what types of stories they run and in which sections of the paper or magazine you might fit. Most major papers have a Lifestyles section, as well as Metro and Business sections, and the ever-popular Food section. Target the section in which you would like to appear and tailor your approach accordingly.

Once you obtain publicity, make the most of it. Quote commentary in your brochures (e.g., " 'Fabulous' says *The Miami Herald*" or "*The Chicago Tribune* calls it the 'Best buy west of the Mississippi' "). Photocopy the article and include it in your promotional materials. It's always easier to let someone else do the bragging for you! If you manage to get an entire article devoted to you, make reprints and distribute them to everyone on your mailing list.

■ *Press releases*. Call the local newspaper and find out what its criteria are for news releases. If you've been in business for three years and are simply looking for press coverage, don't count on it. But if you're just starting out or branching into new areas, especially if you offer a service to the general public, newspapers are often responsive. A news release is usually a straightforward, one-page story or description about an event or product. It has the tone of a news article, with few flowery adjectives.

Compose a release and mail it to the appropriate editor, along with a cover letter, black-and-white photos of you or your product, and samples, where appropriate (who wouldn't love to receive free brownies?).

■ *Promotions*. A promotion is any special event you host to publicize your business, such as a grand opening, party, open house or participation in large-scale events. The key to successful promotions is assuring everyone that free food and prizes will be on hand. The lure of freebies may garner some publicity for your business.

■ *Seminars and workshops*. Contact local adult education programs in your area and indicate your availability and credentials to present workshops and seminars. You might also offer to speak for local community groups, free of charge, if necessary. Remember, in these contexts, you will be selling yourself and your knowledge, not necessarily your product or service. But you will receive exposure and the hope for future business.

I recently made a phone call to the local adult school and indicated my availability to conduct evening workshops on working at home. As it turned out, they were very interested. I'll soon be teaching my first class. Doing so will not only enable me to earn a respectable hourly income, it will also provide me with additional exposure to the community.

■ *Talk shows*. Getting on "Good Morning America" may be beyond your reach (then again, remember Marcia Cone-Esaki from chapter 1?). But local television and radio stations run talk shows on a daily basis. Did you ever stop to think where they find guests, day after day? How are those guests selected? Station managers or other staff are paid to find experts and interesting people. Just think what a great favor you'll be doing them by offering to lend your presence to their show. If you have something interesting to say and are able to express yourself well, go for it!

Be sure to express your appreciation to those individuals who provide publicity. Send a thank you note. Building relationships with local media personnel can certainly increase your chances of receiving additional coverage in the future. And everyone appreciates a little kindness.

Networking

Networking involves making specific plans to meet people who can provide you with personal and professional support, useful information and business. When you think of establishing a network, first look to your current circle of friends and business associates. Many of them probably can and will be of service in numerous ways. Perhaps your cousin Bob is a computer salesman. He can give you advice and, hopefully, a great discount. Your former boss might be willing to hire you as a subcontractor when the office is shorthanded. Maybe your next-door neighbor is on the staff of the local newspaper; she may help you get some publicity.

Your current contacts are, more than likely, not sufficient. Like it or not, when it comes to business, *who* you know is often more important than *what* you know. (Be honest now, wouldn't *you* rather do business with someone you know, rather than a total stranger?) So try to get to know as many people as possible. Consider joining organizations such as the local chamber of commerce. Attend seminars and workshops geared to small-business owners or others who may be able to use your service or product.

Trade associations exist for many different fields, such as the American Bar Association, the National Association of Secretarial Services and hundreds of others. There's bound to be one related to your business. Joining will give you the opportunity to meet people who have faced similar struggles and can provide valuable advice.

You may even find that elusive, but very desirable, individual known as a mentor. That's someone who not only has been down the road you're traveling but is willing to share experiences and help you along the way.

Wherever you go, be sure to carry business cards and hand them out liberally. These are small enough that most people are willing to save them, whereas they might toss a brochure or advertisement. And be sure to ask for business cards from people who might be future business associates.

Your notebook (see chapter 3) should contain a section titled "Contacts and Prospects," where you can record the name and address of new contacts you make. You should also have a place to retain business cards. Stationery stores sell special files to hold business cards. You may simply keep them in a small box or staple them onto address cards.

Checking Out the Competition

A discussion of marketing is not complete without considering the number-one obstacle your business must overcome: competition. More than likely, your business will not be entirely unique. That means you will have to deal with competition, so find out all you can about your competitors *before* you open for business.

First, look in the Yellow Pages to find similar businesses. Also, scan newspaper ads and keep your eyes open for flyers and direct mail pieces. If you find competitors, call and ask questions, and request brochures and other material. This information will help you find your own niche in the marketplace.

If you believe you can realistically compete or there is enough business to go around, then you should proceed with your marketing plans. If not, consider some other possibilities until you find your niche.

Questions

1. Is your product or service something people use all the time? Is it practical?

2. If people are not currently using it, can you convince them they ought to? How?

3. Describe the person most likely to buy your product or service.

4. What magazines are your potential customers likely to read? (Look at the *Reader's Guide to Periodical Literature* at your local library or simply peruse a magazine rack for inspiration.)

5. Is your product or service general enough to warrant advertising in the local newspapers? If yes, list those newspapers you plan to contact for advertising information.

6. Where and how have you seen similar products advertised? Begin clipping and filing all competitive ads.

7. Is your product or service the type that would be promoted through a direct mail letter or flyer? If so, develop a sample letter advertising your product. Get feedback from your friends and relatives.

8. Who are your competitors?

9. In what ways are their businesses similar to yours?

10. How will your service or product be better?

11. Do their businesses seem to be growing or declining? Why?

12. Assuming you can offer a competitive product or service, can you do so at a price that makes your effort worthwhile?

Questions About Publicity

1. What is interesting or unique about your product or service?

2. Does your product or service reveal anything about your community or our society?

3. What newspapers and magazines would you like to be featured in? List
    them under "Publication." Obtain several copies of each and study them
    to determine which section you might fit into and the name of the
    appropriate editor or reporter to contact.

    Publication   **Section**   **Contact**

    _____   _____   _____

    _____   _____   _____

    _____   _____   _____

    _____   _____   _____

    _____   _____   _____

    _____   _____   _____

    _____   _____   _____

4. List five ideas for promotional events.

5. List ten friends, relatives or former colleagues who may be able to help
    you, and how.

6. List two local organizations you might consider joining for networking
    purposes. Contact each to obtain more information.

7. Review the list of associations in chapter 19. List those you will contact
    for more information.

Assignments

1. Write a press release.
2. Have photos taken of you and your product, if appropriate.
3. Find out if your community offers an adult school and if they would be
    interested in having you teach a class.

CHAPTER EIGHT

Your Home Office

O ne of the first requirements for a home-based business is finding a place to work. Ideally, you should have a room set aside expressly for this purpose, but of course, that is not always possible. But don't dismay; be creative. When I was a student, my husband and I were living in a small one-bedroom apartment, and a quiet work space was mandatory. Believe it or not, I set up a little table in a closet and used it as my office! Actually, this arrangement worked surprisingly well because I only went in there when I was serious about working. That is one of the most important rules of a good office: use it only for working. That way, you will learn to associate your office with productivity.

Your office may simply be a section of your bedroom or living room set aside exclusively for your use. Perhaps you could fashion a partition to make things look more official. If you take your business seriously, your family and friends will be more inclined to respect your efforts.

Search flea markets if you must (a friend of mine bought a beautiful desk with a typing stand for $7.50 at an auction), in order to set up the basics of an office: a table and chair, calculator, pencil cup, stapler, paper clips, in-out trays and so on.

The best way to keep organized is to create a place for everything. It sounds hackneyed, but it really is much easier to keep things in place that way. Don't clutter your work area with photographs and knick-knacks; put the former on the wall and sell the latter at a yard sale! Strive for a professional appearance.

You should also give careful attention to which colors you select for your office. Research demonstrates that colors actually have a physical affect on the human body. Red, for example, increases blood pressure and is associated with energy and stimulation. So if you need a boost to get going, buy some red cloth for curtains, a wall-hanging or whatever. Yellow is a bright, cheerful color, so you may want splashes of yellow in your work area—a dried flower arrangement, table cloth, etc.

If you tend to be hyperactive and your work requires a relaxed frame of mind, blue and green are associated with reduced blood pressure, relaxation and tranquility. My carpet and desk are both light blue.

Avoid blacks, browns, grays and earth tones. These are not only associated with fatigue and sedated behavior but actually make the available space seem smaller. White, on the other hand, is a neutral color that increases the perception of space. It's hard to go wrong with white or off-white walls. By the way, any money you spend fixing up your office is completely tax deductible (see chapter 11).

Once you've established your office, all that remains is to make good use of it. One very practical approach is to hold office hours during the same time each day, if at all possible. During this time, the family knows not to disturb you unless something urgent comes up. Your office hours may be before the children wake up, during nap time or after they are in bed at night. Or you may train the children to read, do homework or play quietly during your work hours.

Try to maintain a log to record the date, number of hours worked and the project you worked on. When the time comes to bill clients or price your products, this will provide a basis for calculating costs. The important thing is that you work *a little each day*, rather than allowing projects to accumulate. And again, only sit in your office when you want to work.

Your Desk

You will be spending many hours at your desk, so it pays to invest some thought and planning into making it right from the start. Purchase the most comfortable desk and chair you can afford. If you're a mother, you have enough things wearing you down without having to endure back and neck strain from working in an uncomfortable position. Your increased efficiency will pay for the desk several times over.

As with your office in general, avoid clutter on your desk. As a rule of thumb, if you don't use an item at least once a day, it doesn't belong on top of your desk. Staplers, tape dispensers and the like are wonderful gadgets, but if all they do is occupy space, let them be wonderful in a drawer somewhere.

Essential Equipment

The equipment you require will depend upon the type of business you have. A clown company probably can't get by without a helium-balloon dispenser, a dog breeder will need to purchase cages, and a free-lance photographer will want darkroom equipment. But certain equipment will benefit virtually any business.

■ *Telephone*. There are several reasons you may want to consider installing a separate business telephone line. First, doing so enables you to list your business in the Yellow Pages, which is an important advertising medium. Second, when the phone rings, you can be sure it is business-related and answer the call appropriately. If you have children, you can instruct them not to answer your business phone (older children may be an exception). Third, you can avoid publicizing your *home* phone number on business cards, advertisements and brochures.

Today, phone companies offer a wide variety of services that may be beneficial. If your business receives a high volume of incoming calls, you may want to install call waiting. You may even want to invest in several lines, with a hold button, if warranted. Customers who are met with a busy signal or continuous ringing are likely to take their business elsewhere. Remember, saving money in the short run may cost you in the long run.

■ *Answering machine*. These can be purchased for under fifty dollars and are well worth the investment if incoming calls constitute a major avenue of business development. If you have commitments that require you to be away from home for long periods of time, you can't afford *not* to purchase one.

■ *Computer*. Personal computers are becoming as commonplace in American homes as televisions. They can enhance both your efficiency and professional image. Of course, the nature of your business will determine whether you need a computer. (See chapter 9 for a complete discussion.)

■ *Typewriter*. In many cases, computers have rendered the typewriter obsolete (it's still easier to *type* an envelope, though!). Depending on your business, however, a typewriter may be sufficient. Or if you cannot afford a computer, you may want to obtain an electronic typewriter (they are fairly easy to come by secondhand). All correspondence sent out from your home office should be typed. In the long run, typing it yourself will save you money.

■ *Filing cabinet*. No matter what line of business you enter, paper is bound to flow in and out of your office. Government forms, financial records, customer information and invoices all need to be retained in an orderly fashion. Fireproof metal cabinets are a wise investment, but they can be expensive. Again, you may find one secondhand. In the meantime, you can use cardboard filing boxes or heavy plastic containers, available at any stationery store.

Organizing a Filing System

As a general rule, try to throw away more than you file, otherwise you'll drown in a sea of paper. Only save what you really need. For example, don't save an entire magazine; save only the article of interest to you. Of course, some things will certainly need to be saved for retrieval at a later time. Some suggested file categories are listed below.

■ *Subject file*. The best way to set up your initial subject files, according to Robert Scott, author of *Office at Home*, is by labeling a series of file folders

A-Miscellaneous through Z-Miscellaneous. That way, you can create specific subject files as warranted. For instance, once your G-Miscellaneous file has accumulated five letters from George's Paper Supply, you can make a subject file especially for it.

Another approach is to set up temporary files by marking folders in pencil. Affix a typed label only when you are certain you need a file for that particular subject. It doesn't make sense to make a separate file for every piece of paper you want to keep. If you do, you'll have a hundred files within a few weeks.

Eventually, you should have a file (by company or individual name) for every major customer or vendor you do business with. You should also make subject files for special projects you are working on or topics that relate to your business. For example, you may be developing a new product line to add to your mail-order business. Make a special file and put everything pertaining to it in one place (regardless of who the vendor is). Or you may hope to write a book someday on child rearing. If you come across helpful articles from time to time, file them all in one subject folder, rather than by author or some other means.

File folders and labels are both available in a wide variety of colors, so you may consider color-coding your system. For example, vendors may be in yellow folders, clients in blue folders, projects in green folders and so on. Alternatively, you may opt to use all manila folders with different colored labels.

■ *Chronological file*. You should maintain a copy of all correspondence sent out from your office in date order. The best approach is to three-hole punch each document and store it in a binder. Once the binder is full, mark the beginning and ending dates on the side of the binder and start a new one.

■ *Tickler file*. These files are designed to bring papers to your attention when needed, no sooner and no later. There are two primary methods for this. The first is a folder or binder with index tabs numbered one through thirty-one, representing each day of the month. On any given day, you can open the file to the appropriate date, reminding you of invoices that need to be paid and other important items.

The second approach is to maintain a binder, similar to your chronological file. Write in pencil the date you'll need a particular piece of paper on the upper right-hand corner, three-hole punch it and place it in the binder (the most recent date in front). Each morning, simply open the binder to determine if there is anything marked with today's date. This is a great way to keep track of sales leads.

Supplies

Each office has unique requirements, which will become self-evident as time passes. Don't rush out and spend a fortune on unnecessary supplies. Start with only the basics and build your inventory in the months ahead. The following list of commonly needed office supplies will serve as a guide:

Address book or file	Paper clips
Business card holder	Pencil holder
Correction fluid	Pencil sharpener
Desk organizer	Postage scale
Drawer Organizer	Postage stamps
Envelopes	Ruler
File folders and labels	Rubber bands
Glue	Scissors
Hole-punch	Scotch tape
In and out boxes	Stapler and staples
Letter opener	Three-ring binders

Stationery

As previously mentioned, stationery is an important part of your overall marketing strategy. Potential clients are likely to base their first impression of you on correspondence they receive, so make it a positive one. If you cannot afford to buy everything at once, start with business cards first, and then move on to letterhead, brochures and so on. Ideally, you should hire a professional graphic designer to create a distinctive logo for your company.

But be forewarned, this can be expensive. You may be able to employ the services of a friend with artistic experience or a graphic design student.

■ *Business cards*. These are an integral part of everyday business affairs. They are exchanged at both formal and informal meetings, and represent an inexpensive and lasting form of advertising. On average, five hundred cards cost twenty-five to fifty dollars. So for about five or ten cents, you can obtain an almost permanent place in the business card file of a potential customer.

Since they are so affordable, don't settle for the bottom of the line. Get professional-looking card stock and a design that reflects who you are and what your business is about. A business card should include the name of your company, your name, address and phone number. If you have a logo or slogan, include that as well. If not, you may want to include a list of services provided. Various colors, textures, type styles, graphic designs and paper weights are available, so explore all the possibilities.

■ *Letterhead*. Your letterhead should be printed on the same color paper, using the same logo, slogan, type style and graphic design as your business card. Again, choose quality bond paper to ensure a professional-looking result. If you have a laser printer and want to avoid the expense of letterhead, you can design your own and print it on plain bond paper each time you send out correspondence.

■ *Brochures, flyers and invoices*. Like letterhead, any brochures, flyers or invoices sent out from your office should share the same logo, slogan, type style and graphic design. A consistent, uniform design looks professional and will be memorable. This will help develop an image for your company in the minds of potential customers as they become visually familiar with you.

Procedures Manual

Outline the tasks you perform on a regular basis, listing exactly what is involved with getting each task done. Be as detailed as possible. Write it as if you were explaining it so someone else could take over the assignment. Hopefully, one day you'll be able to delegate some of the easier tasks, and you'll be glad you took the time to write out explanations. Also, write down the format that should be followed for all correspondence out of your office, including letters, invoices and advertisements.

Questions

1. Where will you set up your office?

2. List the equipment you will need to get started and ideas for obtaining it.

3. Note your office hours for each day:

    Monday
    Tuesday
    Wednesday
    Thursday
    Friday
    Saturday

    (Why not make a large "Mom Working" sign and post it on your office door? Begin holding office hours *today*!)

4. List the office supplies you will need. Begin to purchase them, one by one if necessary.

Assignments

1. Purchase your supplies and equipment.
2. Set up your filing system.
3. Once you've decided on a company name, have your stationery printed. If you can afford it, hire a professional to design a logo for you or contact a local art school.

CHAPTER NINE

Do You Need a Computer?

Thanks to the increasing affordability of personal computers, many home-based businesswomen ought to consider buying one. However, don't rush out to buy a computer until you've determined that you really do need one and understand what you need it for.

The nature of the work you do is the first criterion to examine. Some jobs lend themselves better to computerization than others. You don't need a computer to crochet baby sweaters, but publishing a newsletter with one will save you time, money and headaches. In certain professions, a computer is almost mandatory. Secretaries, writers, salespeople and anyone else whose business survival demands storing and manipulating information can enhance their productivity with a computer.

Also consider the volume of work that could be computerized. Your home-based crocheting business probably wouldn't require a computer if you are only making three sweaters every month to sell at the local bazaar. But if you are selling hundreds of sweaters via mail, a computer would help maintain a list of customers. That's extremely important because in the mail-order business, your best prospects for future sales are those who have bought from you in the past and know the quality of your products.

Second, you must determine what you need a computer for. If you type only one letter a week, a typewriter would probably suffice. If, on the other hand, you need to keep track of inventory, pay bills, issue invoices or work with columns of numbers for other reasons, a computer can help. Maintaining a list of previous, existing or prospective customers will be more simple and efficient with a computer. Today's computers can even help artists, cross-stitchers, fashion designers, architects and other professionals with software programs designed for creative projects.

Gloria Ghedini of Ghedini Group Tours has found that using a computer has revolutionized her travel service. "It used to take me hours of phone calls to obtain flight schedules, and often the information was wrong anyway," she says. Today, using her computer to access the Sabre System, Gloria can get immediate, up-to-date details on flight times and rates, car rentals, hotels and more.

Before You Buy

Before you spend hundreds or even thousands of dollars, think through your purchase carefully and research which computer system is best for you. Once you've determined that you really do need a computer, you must decide *where* to buy. Ask yourself the following questions:

■ *Is the vendor reputable?* Be sure the store or individual who sells you the hardware and software is willing to back it up. Have they been in business long? Does it seem like they'll be in business for a long time to come? Talk to people who have dealt with the vendor. Are they happy with the equipment and service? Beware of outfits that look fly-by-night even if they offer a seemingly better deal than a more reputable dealer.

■ *Is one-stop shopping available?* Unless you (or someone you trust) are a computer expert, you're probably better off dealing with a store that offers a wide variety of hardware and software. A representative will help you put together a complete package, including computer, printer, software and accessories. Some computer stores carry only one line of computers. Unbiased advice is more common at diversified stores.

■ *What support services are available?* When it comes to service, be sure to ask questions and get the answers in writing. Find out in advance if the store backs up the products they sell. If you get home and can't figure out how to set things up, can you call for help or are you on your own the minute you walk out the door? If the printer breaks down three months from now, what do you do? What if it breaks down three years from now?

More than likely, the salesman will try to sell you a service contract (which picks up where the warranty leaves off) along with your hardware. Take it home and think it over. If computer equipment is the backbone of your business and neither you nor anyone you know is proficient with computers, a service contract may not be a bad idea. But shop around. If a nearby computer repair shop offers reasonable prices, you can use their service when needed without paying an annual fee. In fact, the price of computer hardware is dropping so rapidly that replacement is often cheaper than repair.

■ *Is the model you want user-friendly?* Virtually all computer companies insist that their product is easy to use. Before you buy, make sure you agree with your salesperson's definition of *easy*. Most dealers will let you try out merchandise in the store. Set aside several hours to test-drive hardware and software. You might even want to come back several times, taking notes each time. Take a look at the manual. If it looks like you'd need a Ph.D. in computer science to understand it, choose a different product. Companies with unfriendly manuals usually have unfriendly products.

■ *Is tutorial software included?* If you have no prior experience with a particular software program, be sure the package includes a tutorial program (a computerized tutor that will instruct you at your own pace). Of course, you'll be anxious to dive right in when you bring home the "baby," but you'll be spared much frustration if you take the time to work through the tutorial at least once before attempting the real thing.

■ *Is there a hot line?* The availability of a toll-free hot line is an important factor to consider, especially when purchasing a printer or software package.

Invariably, questions arise during the course of daily use that lend themselves to solution over the phone. If you are a novice, a toll-free help line could make the difference between survival and madness!

■ *Which operating system does your model run on?* The operating system your computer uses will determine which software packages you can use. This is why you should choose software first. Most IBM and IBM-compatible computers use a version of MS-DOS or Windows. I recommend you give serious consideration to purchasing an MS-DOS system, because it is so widely used and almost certain to remain popular.

However, Apple, Commodore and Tandy are just a few of the very popular home computers on the market that do not use MS-DOS. If you are interested in graphics capabilities or desktop publishing, Apple Macintosh is widely regarded as an excellent choice. Try to find an unbiased computer consultant to help you make the decision.

Hardware

Hardware is the backbone of any computer system. This includes the diskdrive, monitor, keyboard and printer. The most important factor to look for is expandability. Will the system grow with you? Will you be able to upgrade as new technologies become available? Another key component is compatibility (see discussion on operating systems). Make sure the software you need now, and the software you think you might want in the future, will run on the hardware. You also need to ensure that your hardware is compatible with hardware you may add later.

Personal computers have revolutionized American society, and they can do the same for your business. But be sure to think through carefully what features you need before you spend a lot of money for a system too advanced for your needs.

Some things you need to know about personal computers include the following:

Memory

Memory is measured in kilobytes, and the size of your computer's memory will determine how much information can be stored on it. You can always increase the amount of memory in your computer later on, so you may want to start with the standard level of memory included with your computer.

Storage

The two primary modes of storing information are on a hard drive and floppy disks. The hard drive is an internal unit able to store data within the computer itself. Floppy disks are inserted into the computer disk drives.

Floppies come in various sizes, the most common sizes being three-and-a-half and five-and-a-quarter inches. A few years ago, five-and-a-fourth-inch diskettes were by far the most popular, but the three-and-a-half-inch diskette is becoming more common. These smaller disks have an outer shell of rigid plastic and are sturdier and less temperamental than the larger ones.

For most documents, storage on a diskette is sufficient. However, for large or important documents, keep a backup copy on the hard drive or make an extra copy on another diskette.

Monitors

The monitor is the part of the computer that looks like a television screen; it is the window into your computer. Choose one that is adjustable. You'll want to be able to tilt the monitor in various directions to avoid glare coming through the window or from a light. If other members of your family use the computer, they'll want to adjust it to suit their eye level. Adjustability is also important to prevent neck strain.

Two main types of monitors are available on the market today: monochrome and color. Monochrome monitors usually have a dark gray or green background with bright lettering. Color monitors offer virtually limitless combinations of background and foreground colors. Monochrome monitors are far less expensive than color and are sufficient for most business uses. However, if your business is art-related, it's worth the extra money to buy a color display.

Keyboards

The keyboard, as you would expect, resembles a typewriter. Before you buy, test-drive the keyboard to make sure you are comfortable with it. Some keyboards are so tiny and the keys so close together that you can hit A, S, D and F keys all at the same time with one stroke of your pinky finger.

The tactile resistance or "touch" of the keyboard is also important. If you've been using a manual typewriter for twenty years, you might feel comfortable with a heavier touch. On the other hand, if you are accustomed to typing at a rapid pace, a lighter touch is probably preferable. Chances are, you'll be spending many hours at the keyboard; do everything you can to ensure that they'll be as painless as possible.

You might also want to consider buying a freestanding keyboard rather than one that is attached to the computer unit. These can be placed on your lap or anywhere else you feel like putting them, so you could conceivably type lying on the couch with the computer behind you (this is a fine art, so don't expect it to blossom overnight!).

Printers

Unlike typewriters, computers require a two-step process to produce a document. First, you create the document on the computer, then you print it out on paper. The printer that's right for you depends upon the quality and volume of documents you plan to produce. The three major categories of printers are:

■ *Letter quality*. These work much like a typewriter, using a ball or daisy wheel unit to impact a ribbon, making an impression on the paper. Generally speaking, they are rather slow and loud, but the final result looks exactly like a typed document.

■ *Dot matrix*. This type of printer also relies on the impact method, like typewriters. The difference is that the impressions are formed with a series of dots, which enables the printer to form not only letters but graphic patterns as well.

Another advantage of dot matrix printers is that you can run them in two different modes. Draft mode prints very fast. In letter-quality mode, the printhead makes a second pass per line, putting more dots on each line. Depending upon the manufacturer and model, some dot matrix printers produce high quality documents in letter-quality mode. Years ago, dot matrix printers were very noisy and often slow. Today's models are much improved.

■ *Laser.* This type of printer looks and acts more like a copy machine than a typewriter. Laser printers enable you to print a variety of typefaces and sizes on a single page—from very small to very large. This capability is particularly important for resumés and newsletters, but even an ordinary letter becomes eye-catching when printed with a variety of typefaces.

If you are planning to open a secretarial or resume-writing service, consider purchasing a laser printer. They are far more expensive than the other kinds, but it's even more expensive to lose business because your equipment is not state-of-the-art.

Software

While hardware constitutes the backbone of a computer system, it's the software that "fleshes it out." The software you install on your computer is what makes it uniquely suited to your needs; it's the personal side of the personal computer. A wide array of software programs exist, ranging from daily planners to complete accounting systems. Walking into a software store can make you feel like a kid in a candy shop. But the wise woman will restrict her purchases to those packages she truly needs.

Word Processors

You'll almost certainly need a good word processing package. Whether you're planning to be a free-lance writer or just compose letters to potential customers, life will be much easier without having to fuss over a typewriter. Word processors allow you to change a document an unlimited number of times. As a result, you'll be inclined to let ideas flow more freely, knowing you can always go back and change them later.

Word processors also make it possible to print multiple copies of the same document, so you don't have to retype a standard letter over and over. It also means you can send out customized, high-quality documents rather than impersonal photocopies. This is accomplished through the "merge" feature. That is, you compose your letter, type the names and addresses of everyone you want to send it to, then press a few buttons. The computer will merge the names and addresses into the proper place in your letter, creating individual, personalized copies for each of your clients or customers. Before you know it, you'll have dozens, hundreds, even thousands of customized letters completed.

Most word processors come equipped with an internal dictionary. Press a button, and the computer checks for spelling errors. When it finds a possible error, it will point it out to you (each program does so in a different manner) and offer several ways to correct it. If your spelling is poor, by all means invest in a spell-checker or buy a word processor that includes one.

Another product on the market is the grammar-checker, usually sold separately. If your grammar is worse than your spelling, and you can afford it, you might buy one of these as well.

Be sure to purchase a word processing package that is widely used, particularly in your target industry. WordPerfect and Microsoft Word are widely used in most corporate environments, while WordStar is popular in academic circles. No matter what a "deal" it seems like, resist the temptation to buy an unknown software package just because the price is right.

Database Management Systems

Database management systems do exactly what the name implies—they enable you to manage data. They are most useful for maintaining large mailing lists or product information. Your database will enable you to retrieve detailed information with the touch of a few buttons.

Let's assume you input the name, address and item purchased for every customer, as well as a note about how they heard of your business. You can then ask the computer to show you all your customers by last name in alphabetical order, or those who live in Detroit or everyone who purchased Product A, or everyone who heard of your business through a certain newspaper ad. This information will help you make decisions about where to advertise and what type of people to target.

Financial Applications

There are many software programs that can help you manage the financial side of your business. If you want to add columns and rows of numbers, you'll need a spreadsheet, which looks just like a columnar pad, except that the computer does the math for you. Spreadsheets are available in many configurations and applications. Lotus 1-2-3 and QuattroPro are two of the most popular spreadsheets.

If you want a program to help you manage your business and personal finances, or if you plan to start a bookkeeping service, you can buy personal finance software. Some of the more popular brands include Quicken, MoneyCounts, Managing Your Money, and Dollars & Sense. If you are looking for very affordable software, one place to try is Parsons Technology (1-800-779-6000). Founded as a home-based business by Bob and Martha Parsons, this company now offers a wide variety of excellent programs in a price range of twenty-nine to forty-nine dollars.

Questions

1. List all your business tasks that lend themselves to computerization. (Note: Take this list with you to the computer shop. It will help determine which hardware and software packages you should buy.)

2. As you shop for computers, use the Computer Shopping Assessment form on the following pages to help compare vendors, hardware and software. The checklist will help you determine which features best suit you.

Computer Shopping Assessment

	Vendors		
	Vendor #1	Vendor #2	Vendor #3
Reputable	Yes ☐ No ☐	Yes ☐ No ☐	Yes ☐ No ☐
One-stop shopping	Yes ☐ No ☐	Yes ☐ No ☐	Yes ☐ No ☐
Support services	Yes ☐ No ☐	Yes ☐ No ☐	Yes ☐ No ☐
Technical assistance	Yes ☐ No ☐	Yes ☐ No ☐	Yes ☐ No ☐
Repair service	Yes ☐ No ☐	Yes ☐ No ☐	Yes ☐ No ☐

	Hardware		
	Brand #1	Brand #2	Brand #3
User-friendly	Yes ☐ No ☐	Yes ☐ No ☐	Yes ☐ No ☐
Tutorial included	Yes ☐ No ☐	Yes ☐ No ☐	Yes ☐ No ☐
Hot line	Yes ☐ No ☐	Yes ☐ No ☐	Yes ☐ No ☐
Compatible with software	Yes ☐ No ☐	Yes ☐ No ☐	Yes ☐ No ☐
Which operating system			

	Software		
	Word Processing		
	Program #1	Program #2	Program #3
Word Processor			
User-friendly	Yes ☐ No ☐	Yes ☐ No ☐	Yes ☐ No ☐
Tutorial	Yes ☐ No ☐	Yes ☐ No ☐	Yes ☐ No ☐
Hot line	Yes ☐ No ☐	Yes ☐ No ☐	Yes ☐ No ☐
Compatible with software	Yes ☐ No ☐	Yes ☐ No ☐	Yes ☐ No ☐

Database Manager

	Program #1	Program #2	Program #3
User-friendly	Yes ☐ No ☐	Yes ☐ No ☐	Yes ☐ No ☐
Tutorial	Yes ☐ No ☐	Yes ☐ No ☐	Yes ☐ No ☐
Hot line	Yes ☐ No ☐	Yes ☐ No ☐	Yes ☐ No ☐
Compatible	Yes ☐ No ☐	Yes ☐ No ☐	Yes ☐ No ☐

Spreadsheet

	Program #1	Program #2	Program #3
User-friendly	Yes ☐ No ☐	Yes ☐ No ☐	Yes ☐ No ☐
Tutorial	Yes ☐ No ☐	Yes ☐ No ☐	Yes ☐ No ☐
Hot line	Yes ☐ No ☐	Yes ☐ No ☐	Yes ☐ No ☐
Compatible	Yes ☐ No ☐	Yes ☐ No ☐	Yes ☐ No ☐

Financial Planner

	Program #1	Program #2	Program #3
User-friendly	Yes ☐ No ☐	Yes ☐ No ☐	Yes ☐ No ☐
Tutorial	Yes ☐ No ☐	Yes ☐ No ☐	Yes ☐ No ☐
Hot line	Yes ☐ No ☐	Yes ☐ No ☐	Yes ☐ No ☐
Compatible	Yes ☐ No ☐	Yes ☐ No ☐	Yes ☐ No ☐

CHAPTER TEN

Legal Issues

Many potential home-based entrepreneurs are scared off by legal hurdles and red tape. I won't sugarcoat things by telling you that legalities and paperwork are not a hassle. However, the amount of red tape will be determined by the size, complexity and nature of your business. In fact, most home businesses require very little paperwork.

On the other hand, if you are starting big and will be hiring employees, you should seek the advice of a professional lawyer who specializes in small businesses. You will need to ensure compliance with the Fair Labor Standards Act, the Consumer Product Safety Act and the Occupational Safety and Health Act, just to name a few. The Small Business Administration (SBA) or trade associations related to your industry can also answer any questions you have.

Choosing a Legal Structure

The first legal decision you will have to make is what type of structure your business will assume. Each of the four options are discussed in this section.

■ *Sole proprietorship*. This offers substantial benefits for the home-based businesswoman, and in the vast majority of instances this structure should be chosen. You will not incur any legal fees, because there are no forms to file. You simply register with the city or county clerk, as discussed below, a task you can certainly do without legal assistance. It's important to consider that sole proprietors are permitted to employ their spouses and children without paying Social Security or Federal Unemployment Taxes. That is not the case for a corporation. Chances are, your family will end up on the payroll at some point, so this is an important benefit.

Another factor to consider, which is both an advantage and a disadvantage, is that a sole proprietorship can close its doors at any time. That's good if you have truly given your home business your best shot and things just haven't worked out—or if you've earned so much money that you can retire early. It's not so good, however, when you are tempted to throw in the towel without allowing enough time for your business to develop.

Under a sole proprietorship, all profits and losses are attributed to you personally. So if your business will involve taking major financial risks, you should seriously consider adopting a corporate structure. Otherwise, you will just need to file a Schedule C, "Profit or Loss from Business or Profession," when you file your 1040 Form at the end of the year. If you earn more than four hundred dollars, you will also have to file a Schedule SE, "Social Security Self-Employment Tax."

■ *Partnership*. The tax ramifications of a partnership are very similar to a sole proprietorship, except that partners split the income or loss reported on their respective 1040 Forms at the end of each year. Many states have a Uniform Partnership Act that defines a partnership as "an association of two or more persons to carry on as co-owners of a business for profit" (SBA publication: *Selecting the Legal Structure for Your Firm*).

A partnership can be based on a verbal agreement, but a written document is a wise precaution. Some of the things you should spell out in a written partnership agreement include:

1. Allocation of profits and losses (e.g., fifty-fifty, sixty-forty)

2. Salary provisions
3. Capital to be invested by each party
4. Provisions for the death or disability of one of the partners
5. Terms relating to the termination of the partnership

■ *Corporation*. A legal corporation is by far the most complex structure your home-based business can assume. If you are planning to hire a large number of employees, then you will have to incorporate your business. Some other factors to consider include better pension and profit-sharing options for your employees; group insurance rates (the premiums for which are fully deductible for the first fifty thousand dollars of coverage); and medical benefits, also fully deductible. In addition, there are capital gains tax benefits available to corporations, which are not available to individuals or partnerships. The first step in this process is to hire a lawyer or accountant.

■ *Sub S Corporation*. The Sub S Corporate structure can be used if your business will show a loss. By applying for Sub S status, you can obtain certain tax benefits. Be sure to consult a tax expert if you think you may qualify.

Choosing and Registering a Name

If you elect to operate as a sole proprietor, you are permitted by law to operate under your own name. However, if presenting a professional image is important to you, then it is advisable to choose an official name for your business. Also, keep in mind that banks will not allow you to open a business account until you have a registration certificate in hand.

When choosing a name, be sure it can grow with you. The name Apples-R-Us may seem cute now, but what if you start selling oranges? On the other hand, if you are a toy maker and won't be expanding into other areas, a name that clearly identifies what you do is best. Contact your county clerk's office to learn the procedures for obtaining a "doing business as" or trade name.

Post Office Box

When you register your trade name, you will be asked to provide a business address. Keep in mind that this address will become public knowledge and within several days, you can expect to receive a truckload of mail from people who want to sell you products and services. It may be advisable to open a post office box in your company's name to prevent the dissemination of your home address.

Sales Tax

Most state governments (and many municipalities) levy a sales tax on merchandise. If you sell or resell a product, you will need a sales authorization certificate. This assigns you a resale tax number so you can buy material wholesale and not have to pay sales tax on it until it is resold, either incorporated into your final product or as is.

You must collect sales tax on everything you sell *directly* to consumers, then remit the money to the appropriate government office. The percentage varies from state to state, so contact your State Department of Taxation, Sales Tax Bureau, for more details.

Licenses and Permits

Depending on the nature of your business, your state or local government may require you to obtain certain licenses or permits before you begin operation. For example, a hairstylist requires a license, and day-care facilities may need special permits. If you are unsure of the requirements for your particular line of business, contact the Small Business Administration or your trade association.

Zoning Regulations

Most states, counties and municipalities have zoning restrictions on the types of businesses that may be conducted in certain areas. You may not be permitted to board horses or open a beauty salon in your housing complex. There is usually a zoning office at county headquarters or city hall. You may also be able to contact your State Office of Economic Development to obtain material outlining restrictions on home-based businesses on a state level. Again, if in doubt, contact your local Small Business Administration office.

Insurance

Be sure to contact your insurance agent to discuss necessary changes to your policy. This is particularly important if you plan to invest in office equipment or will need to maintain inventory in your home. Some of the issues you should discuss include:

1. Fire, theft and casualty damage to equipment and inventory
2. Liability coverage for customers, vendors or others who may visit your home business
3. Product liability coverage if you make or sell a product
4. Professional liability if you will be offering a service
5. Additional car insurance if you will be using your family vehicle for business purposes

Your insurance agent will almost certainly require a copy of your business plan (see chapter 6). Also, be sure to ask if you are entitled to a discount on your homeowner's policy, since working at home much of the time reduces the chance of fire and burglary.

Questions

1. Which legal structure will you assume?

2. List ten possible names for your business. Now begin to narrow it down until you find the *right* one. (Warning: this might take a lot longer than you think. Be sure to get opinions from family and friends as well.)

Assignments

1. Check on zoning laws, if warranted.
2. Open a post office box, if desired.
3. Register your name with the city or county clerk.
4. Apply for applicable licenses or permits.
5. Talk to your insurance agent.

CHAPTER ELEVEN

Finances

Like legal issues, business finances may be unknown territory for the new home-based businesswoman. However, once the terms are understood and a few points clarified, finances become far less daunting. Hopefully, this brief overview will familiarize you with some commonly used financial terms and practices.

Deductible Expenses

When it comes to taxes, you are expected to pay your fair share. Paying more is foolish. As a self-employed businesswoman, you are entitled to certain deductions; don't be afraid to make use of them.

■ *Your home.* If you use part of your home *exclusively* or *regularly* for business, and it serves as your *principal place of business*, you are entitled to deduct costs as a business expense. *Exclusively* means that portion of your home that is used for business and nothing else. You cannot deduct your bedroom or kitchen if you use part of it for business and part of it for family. The deduction is allowable only if you have an entire room set aside for business. The one exception is inventory storage. For example, if you use half of the basement to store products, you can deduct it. You may also deduct for other facilities located on your property, such as a greenhouse, artist's studio or garage, if they are used solely for business purposes. *Regularly* means that even though you don't devote your full time to conducting your business at home, you do so on a regular basis. Your home is your *principal place of business* if you spend more than 50 percent of the time devoted to a particular job at home (in other words, your home can qualify even if your business is a side-job).

The deduction allowed is based on the percentage of your house used. The most acceptable way to determine this is to calculate the square footage of your office as a percentage of the entire square footage of your house. Or you can approximate using the following method: Let's assume you have a three-bedroom house with a dining room, kitchen and living room, and all six rooms are approximately the same size. If one of the rooms serves as your office, you can deduct one-sixth of the mortgage, real estate tax, electricity, homeowners insurance, etc., as a business expense.

■ *Indirect expenses*. Even putting on a new roof, painting the exterior and other such renovations and repairs are all considered indirect expenses related to your business and are partially deductible based on the percentage.

■ *Direct expenses*. Directly related expenses, such as painting or carpeting the office, are fully deductible. However, keep in mind that the total deduction taken for the business use of your home cannot exceed the gross income earned from the business. To simplify your expense recording throughout the year, incorporate the preprinted expense forms (chapter 18) into your personal notebook.

■ *Travel*. Whenever you take a trip for the sole purpose of conducting or promoting your business, all expenses—air fare, car rental, lodging, meals—are fully deductible.

■ *Entertainment and business gifts*. You can also deduct the cost of lunches, dinners, tickets, etc., incurred while cultivating clients or prospects. A five-minute discussion with your best friend about how things are going does not constitute a business lunch. The event must be directly related to the active conduct of your business.

■ *Education and training*. If you attend seminars, classes or conventions to further your business skills, you can deduct fees, tuition and books, as well as transportation and incidental expenses.

■ *Local transportation*. When you run general business errands — to the store or a client's site, for example — you are entitled to deduct mileage, parking and tolls. Or you can deduct a percentage of gas, oil, tires, insurance, repairs or even the cost of a new car. (To determine the correct percentage, keep track of how many miles are used exclusively for business and how many miles were traveled overall throughout the year.) Please note that you cannot have it both ways. You may use either the per mile deduction *or* the percentage method.

■ *Research events*. Any time you take a trip to acquire information necessary for your business, whether it's to the local library or to check out the competition, the expenses you incur are deductible (mileage, parking, library materials, etc.).

■ *Donations*. If you donate one of your products to charity, such as a handcrafted vase, the actual worth (not the sale price) of the item is deductible.

■ *Regular expenses*. Any expenses you incur in the regular course of business are fully deductible, including installation of a telephone (or a percentage of your telephone bill, plus actual business calls), an answering machine, computer or any other equipment. But don't forget the "little" things, which can add up (tape, envelopes, postage, paper clips, pens, stationery). Advertising expenses, business cards and interest payments on loans are also deductible. Whenever possible, pay for business expenses by check and obtain receipts. Taking an extra minute to write an explanation on the back of the receipt will be a tremendous help when tax season rolls around.

When To Pay Taxes

By the time you file your tax return, you should have paid 80 percent of total income tax and Social Security tax due for the year. This is accomplished by filing Form 1040-ES, "Declaration of Estimated Tax," and paying the estimated tax based on how much you have earned over the preceding three months. The deadlines for quarterly filings are January 15, April 15, June 15 and September 15. Your state government may also require quarterly filings.

Employees

If you employ anyone, you are required to obtain Form SS-4 to receive an Employer's Identification Number. You will pay 6.7 percent of the employee's earnings to Social Security and deduct 6.7 percent from the employee's paycheck as well.

Federal Tax Identification Number

You must obtain a Federal Tax Identification Number if you have even one employee at any given point. Once obtained, the IRS will send quarterly and year-end payroll tax returns that must be returned even if you no longer have an employee.

Employee's Withholding Allowance

IRS Form W-4, the employee's withholding allowance, indicates marital status and the number of exemptions to be withheld from each paycheck. This form is filled out by each employee and retained by you as the basis for withholding taxes.

You should contact the Division of Labor Standards, U.S. Department of Labor, for information on minimum wage laws, overtime, discrimination and a host of other matters.

Subcontractors

If you would rather avoid all this red tape, your best bet is to hire independent contractors—that is, people who will work for you on their own time and declare their earnings directly to the government. You do not deduct taxes and are only required to give a Form 1099 to any independent contractor who earns more than six hundred dollars in a given year.

A Word of Warning

Please be aware that tax matters are extremely complex. This section was designed to provide some tips but is by no means intended as a complete guide to taxes. You should consult a tax expert who can help you with your specific questions.

The IRS publication #587 titled *Business Use of Your Home* outlines the income tax regulations specific to a home-based business. The IRS publication *Tax Guide for Small Business* is also very helpful. You can obtain copies of both at your local IRS office.

Record Keeping

The IRS doesn't specify what record keeping format you must use, but you are required by law to retain permanent, accurate and complete records that clearly represent your earnings, deductions and credits. Proper record keeping is an important tool for measuring and enhancing profitability, and it has been proven to increase the likelihood of business success.

According to the Small Business Administration, a good record-keeping system has six primary characteristics:

1. Simple to use
2. Easy to understand
3. Reliable
4. Accurate
5. Consistent
6. Designed to provide information on a timely basis

The components of your system should include a format to track expenses, record income and compare the two. You can purchase a complete record-keeping system, including instructions for its use, at any stationery store. You can also hire an accountant to set up a customized system for you. You may find the forms provided in this book helpful as well. In any case, be sure to include the following:

Cash Disbursements Journal

All expenditures for your business should be recorded in a cash disbursements journal. Don't wait until you have a purse full of receipts before you try to organize them; discipline yourself to record expenses as they are incurred. Your notebook should have a section for "Expenses," along with an envelope for receipts. You can then transfer the information into your detailed journal, which breaks down expenses by category. It should look something like this:

Date	Total $	Description	Supplies	Postage	Advertising
8-5-92	16.22	File Folders	16.22		
8-7-92	50.00	Stamps		50.00	

The categories you need will depend upon your unique business, but they will likely include transportation, entertainment, telephone, utilities, stationery and consulting fees. At the end of each month, total each category. This will give you an excellent idea of where your money is going.

Tracking expenses is easier if you pay for most items using your business checking account. A petty cash fund is also helpful for those occasions when check writing isn't warranted (items under five dollars). You can make up your own petty cash forms or purchase preprinted ones at a stationery store, and use them when a receipt isn't available for small purchases.

Sales Journal

Depending upon the nature of your business, your sales journal may reflect cash register totals on a daily basis or invoices awaiting payment. The first is termed "cash basis" bookkeeping; the latter is called "accrual basis." Cash-based records are straightforward: Carefully record each day's sales totals in a journal.

But if you will be invoicing clients (accrual basis), you should set up a system along the following lines:

Date	Date Rec'd	Customer	Invoice Amount	Product A	B	Sales Tax	Shipping
7-1-92	7-20-92	Stan's Flowers	$34.87	10.00	24.87	$1.67	$2.45
7-2-92	8-3-92	Gifts & Such	$56.88	22.41	34.47	$2.89	$4.78

As you total this information each month, you will learn not only the dollar value of sales but also which products are selling and which are not, so you can adjust your inventory accordingly. You can also see at a glance which customers haven't paid and which customers consistently pay late. You will also know how much sales tax you need to remit to the state. If your shipping expenses are significant, perhaps you can negotiate a volume discount rate with a freight company.

Once you know both your income and expenses, all that remains is to compare the two. Hopefully, income will come out on top every month!

Record Retention

Records that should be kept permanently include cash books, general ledgers, journals, financial statements, audit reports and income tax returns. For six to seven years, you should keep accounts payable and receivable records, canceled checks, inventory records, payroll records, sales receipts and invoices. Records pertaining to payroll taxes should be kept four years.

Budgeting

You will need to develop two types of budgets for your home-based business: start-up and operating. Worksheets for both can be found at the end of this chapter.

Start-Up Costs

The start-up budget is exactly what it sounds like. It represents your best estimates of how much money will be required to get your business underway and includes equipment purchases, phone installation, major office supplies and whatever else you will need to begin. Many of these will be one-time expenses. Once you've determined how much you will need, the next step is to draw upon your savings account, turn to relatives, or if necessary, visit your local bank to discuss a loan.

Operating Budget

This budget projects income and expenses on a month-by-month basis for the first year of operation. Some of the categories you will need to budget for include telephone, office supplies, postage, transportation, entertainment, advertising, professional service fees (accounting and legal), insurance, utilities, taxes and depreciation.

This, of course, is rather difficult to do and you may want to seek the advice of an accountant. The Small Business Administration's Service Corps of Retired Executives (SCORE) staff may also be able to help.

Most experts recommend that you have the equivalent of three to six months' expenditures in reserve, in case your income estimates do not materialize as planned. Do take that into consideration if you are applying for a loan.

Budget Versus Actual

Once you begin operations, each month you should compare how much income you actually earned and how much expenditures you actually incurred with the amounts budgeted for each. If you realize that your budget is unrealistic, you will need to make adjustments accordingly.

Planning is the key to good budgeting, and good budgeting is the key to profitability. Decide not only what you *can* spend (and no more) but what you *will* spend (and no less). One of the hardest things for many people to accept is the reality that they have to spend money to make money. That means taking risks, which is hard. So decide in advance how much you are willing to risk to make your business succeed and then stick to it.

Banking

The key to successful banking is building a relationship with your local banker. Since you have a small business (at least for now), it's best to choose a small, neighborhood bank. As the saying goes, better to be a big fish in a small pond than a small fish in a big pond. Make it a point to get to know the local manager—before you need to ask for a loan.

Checking Accounts

One of the first things you must do is open a checking account. Having a separate business checking account is an excellent way to ensure that good records are kept, because deposits represent your income, and checks or other withdrawals represent your expenses. If you will be conducting business under any name other than your own, be sure to bring your trade-name certificate and several forms of identification.

Before opening a checking account, you should consider some of the following:

1. Is there a minimum deposit required to open the account?
2. What is the waiting period for fund availability on local and out-of-state checks?
3. What are the stop-payment fees?
4. What is the fee for bounced checks?
5. Is there a transaction fee on checks or deposits?
6. Does the bank offer overdraft protection?
7. What service fees, if any, are charged?

Most banks offer discount loan rates to preferred customers, usually meaning anyone who maintains a checking or savings account with the bank. Keep that in mind when deciding where to open your checking account.

Once you have opened your business checking account, treat it with at least as much care as you would your family account. When your monthly statement arrives, reconcile it with your checkbook immediately. If there are any discrepancies, contact your bank. Store canceled checks in an orderly fashion. Keep blank checks in a safe place; they are almost as good as cash to a thief.

Savings Account

If you are a sole proprietor of a small business and will not be writing many checks, you may open a business savings account only. Any checks you do write would be from your personal account. This enables you to avoid paying checking service charges, which can be quite high. In return for some inconvenience, you will even receive interest on your deposits. Check with your accountant to see if this arrangement is best for you.

Automatic Teller Machines

Automatic teller machines (ATMs) make banking convenient. They can be used any time, day or night. Best of all, they are springing up all over—in malls, fast-food restaurants, anywhere you might need emergency cash. Find out if your bank charges a transaction fee for deposits and withdrawals from ATMs, and if so, how much. These can add up over time.

You will also want to find out which ATM network the bank belongs to and be sure there are locations close to your home. If you travel a great deal, make sure the ATM network has locations in the cities or states you frequently visit.

Loans

Banks are in the business of lending money, and they want to lend to you. All they need is a few good reasons to do so. You can greatly improve your chances of obtaining a loan simply by keeping in mind the following tips:

■ *Choose a local bank*. In most instances, a small, community-oriented bank will be much more willing to work with you than a gigantic, city-based financial institution. Don't apologize for operating a small business and don't plead as if the bank is doing you a personal favor. Rest assured that they intend to make a good profit from your loan, however much or little you borrow.

■ *Demonstrate your credibility*. The loan officer sitting behind that desk wants to lend you money; that's how he makes his living. But he needs assurance that you will be able to repay the loan. Your job is to convince him that your business is viable. Provide him with a copy of your business plan. Show him samples or photographs of your products, or provide a copy of a brochure describing your services.

The loan officer wants to talk dollars and cents, so bring your accountant with you. If you don't have one, bring along whoever will be handling the books. If that's you, make sure to brush up on your accounting procedures so you don't look like a novice.

■ *Be prepared to put up collateral*. In other words, if you are unable to repay the loan from your business earnings, you can cash in these items to cover your debt. This is assurance for the bank that they will get their money back, even if your business fails. Savings accounts, stocks and bonds, and your home mortgage are all examples of collateral.

■ *Allow enough time*. Generally speaking, you should allow at least three months from the time you walk into the bank until you actually have the money in hand. And be sure to apply for more money than you think you need, since the bank is almost certain to offer you less than what you apply for.

Assignments

1. Obtain any necessary government forms.
2. Open a business bank account.
3. Apply for loan, if warranted.
4. Complete the projected budget forms on the following pages.

Start-Up Budget

I.   Sources of Funds

1.   Sources: Amount

_____   _____

_____   _____

_____   _____

_____   _____

II.   Uses of Funds

1.   Capital Equipment: Estimated Cost

_____   _____

_____   _____

_____   _____

2.   Office Supplies:

_____   _____

_____   _____

_____   _____

_____   _____

3.   Work Material:

_____   _____

_____   _____

_____   _____

4.   Printed Matter/Advertising:

_____   _____

_____   _____

_____   _____

5.   Other:

_____   _____

_____   _____

_____   _____

First-Year Operating Budget

(Note: You will need to extend this budget out to twelve months using a columnar pad or large piece of paper.)

	January	
	Budget	**Actual**
1. Cash On Hand (Start of month)	_____	_____
2. Cash Received		
Income	_____	_____
Loan	_____	_____
3. Total Cash Available (Total 1 & 2)	_____	_____
4. Disbursements		
a. Office Supplies	_____	_____
b. Postage	_____	_____
c. Telephone	_____	_____
d. Car, Travel	_____	_____
e. Entertainment	_____	_____
f. Advertising/Promotion	_____	_____
g. Accounting, Legal Fees	_____	_____
h. Insurance	_____	_____
i. Utilities	_____	_____
j. Taxes and depreciation	_____	_____
k. Interest	_____	_____
l. Loan Payment	_____	_____
m. Payroll	_____	_____
n. Other (specify):		
_____	_____	_____
_____	_____	_____
Total Cash Paid Out	_____	_____
5. Cash Position (3 minus 4)	_____	_____

Part Three

CONSIDERING THE OPTIONS

CHAPTER TWELVE

Information Technologies

University of Southern California Professor Jack Nilles has coined the term "telecommuting" to describe the phenomenon of people "commuting" to work not by cars but by computers. Alvin Toffler, author of *Future Shock* and *The Third Wave*, predicts an increasing trend toward home-based, technology-based industries, which he termed "electronic cottages." Both of these futurists believe the office and factory will largely disappear as the central place of business becomes the home.

Anyone who spends time commuting to work each morning has a good idea just how much time and energy is wasted in idling or slow-moving automobiles. For example, if you commute just thirty minutes each way, you spend 240 hours per year, or the equivalent of six forty-hour work weeks, on the road.

Another motivation behind the telecommuting phenomenon is concern for the environment. Commuting via computer creates significantly less pollution than driving a car to and from the work place. Another important factor is that America is now largely an information-based economy, and information jobs can be easily transferred to the home. More than 50 percent of all jobs in this

111

country are related to the handling, dissemination, storage and interpreta-
tion of information. Marketing, data processing, bookkeeping, publishing,
insurance and computing are just a few information-based industries that
lend themselves well to home-based businesses.

Thanks to modems, fax machines and advanced telecommunications
capabilities, sitting in your home office is actually more efficient than sitting
in an office downtown. Realizing this, many major corporations are now
actively developing programs to allow their employees to work from home.

Estimates indicate that more than two hundred companies have already
implemented telecommuting programs, involving approximately ten thousand employees. Many more companies are considering this option. If you
are currently employed and think you could perform your duties effectively
from home, why not propose serving as a test case for a corporate telecommuting program?

If you have acquired technical skills that can be transferred from office to
home, you may well be able to find an employer interested in pursuing a
mutually beneficial home-based arrangement. One of the major advantages
of telecommuting is that most companies offer full benefits to their work-at-
home employees.

Refer to Lynie Arden's *Work-at-Home Sourcebook*, which includes information on more than a thousand companies that have home work programs,
with details on job descriptions, pay and benefits, and how to apply.
Positions for word processors, proofreaders, weavers, telemarketers, market
researchers, graphic artists, bookkeepers and many other types of work are
included.

If you have a more entrepreneurial spirit, you can turn your skills into a
free-lance business. Having already developed a solid network of contacts
during your years in the business world, you are well on your way to home-
based business success. According to Georgann Fiumara of the Mothers'
Home Business Network, the tools of technology have become so affordable
that free-lancers are now able to compete with major corporations, both in
terms of pricing and workmanship.

Donna Agnello: Taking Advantage of Technology

Donna Agnello always dreamed of having her own business someday. She grew up in a home attached to the Bucks County Tennis Club, owned and operated by her parents, so she knew the advantages of an entrepreneurial lifestyle. But the road back home has been long and winding.

Donna grew bored with college after two years and decided to relocate from her parents' country home to New York City, with the dream of a music career foremost in her mind. Instead, she landed a job with *Glamour* magazine and worked her way up from secretary to assistant editor.

Along the way, she accumulated a wide variety of skills, including typing, writing, editing, and design and layout. She was surprised to discover she had talents in many of these areas and had never realized it. Donna found herself increasingly intrigued with the marketing-oriented aspects of her job and decided to move in that direction.

She landed a job as public relations director for Peddler's Village, a quaint Pennsylvania town filled with antique and specialty shops. There she handled all aspects of marketing and promotion, from developing brochures to planning radio and print advertisements.

Although Donna enjoyed the work, she had never let go of the dream of being her own boss. So she began to explore, with the help of a career counselor, potential avenues to pursue. After a series of tests to evaluate her skills and interests, she decided that operating a word processing service was her best option.

In February of 1988, with a supportive husband by her side and a ten thousand dollar loan from her parents, Donna invested in state-of-the-art equipment to begin Editype Concepts. She recouped the investment money within the first year. Nevertheless, her earnings were not enough to meet all expenses, so she continued working two days a week for Peddler's Village.

Actually, this worked out well because Donna was able to continue making business contacts through her work for the Village. As a result, Editype Concepts began to evolve. By combining various aspects of both careers, Donna discovered a more interesting and lucrative line of work.

Today, Donna has a new approach to her business, and it appears she's found a useful niche. "I think of myself as a small businessman's ad agency," she says. "They don't have the budget to hire a large agency, and I've got the skills and technology to be their one-stop shop." Since her computer system has desktop publishing capabilities, Donna is able to create newsletters, brochures and advertisements for her clients. And thanks to her media placement experience, she can then help clients use the documents she creates in promotional campaigns.

There is, however, a down side to Donna's business. "If there is one thing that I absolutely detest, it's having to drum up business," she says. "I enjoy *doing* the work; it's *finding* it that I hate." Which is why she has focused her attention on expanding services to existing clients rather than searching for new ones.

Nevertheless, she knows that networking is an important business development tool. She has joined several businesswomen's groups and the chamber of commerce, and it has paid off. Through her various affiliations, Donna has found new clients for her one-stop shop.

Donna offers a word of warning for women considering starting a home-based business: "I would recommend that they thoroughly research their idea and make sure there is a market for it. They must have a goal or plan. The biggest failure for people who start a new business is trying to 'wing it' without doing any homework."

Donna would like to see Editype Concepts grow into a full-fledged ad agency and is working hard to make that happen. In recent days, she has also turned her entrepreneurial sites back to where it all began—the Bucks County Tennis Club. Her parents are now close to retirement, and there is nothing they want more than to leave the business they founded twenty-one years ago as a legacy to their daughter. Although children are not in the forecast for Donna right now, who knows? Maybe a third generation of Agnellos will come to enjoy the many benefits of running a home-based business.

CHAPTER THIRTEEN

Service Industries

Y ears ago, most American jobs were related to the manufacturing industry—in other words, *making* things to sell. Now the Japanese make
everything! But not to fear, Americans have discovered the value of *doing*
things! Today, service-based industries constitute a substantial portion of the
United States' economy.

A service is anything you can do for others because they are unwilling or
unable to do it for themselves. It can be taking care of their dog while they're on
vacation, watching their children while they're at work or cleaning their
bathroom while they watch TV. The bottom line is this: Are you willing to do it
and are people willing to pay you? If the answer to both questions is yes, you've
got a viable business venture on your hands.

A major advantage of starting a service business is that most require lots of
"sweat equity" but a minimal amount of financial risk. That's because, in most
instances, *you* are the only equipment you need. Of course, you may have to obtain
special training or certification, and you might need to purchase some tools of the
trade. But generally speaking, service industries require little up-front investment.

If you would like to start a home-based service, the best approach is to ask people what types of things they don't have the time or inclination to do—but *must* be done. Or simply make a list of the things you wish someone else would do for you: cook, clean, chauffeur your children, go to the grocery store.

Next, target your marketing to people who can afford to hire someone else to do such tasks on their behalf. For the most part, service industries are geared to middle- and upper- class prospects. Be particularly alert to people who are busy or image-conscious. That means business executives and professionals should be foremost in your mind when conjuring up service possibilities.

To give you an illustration, recall that we listed cooking on the list of time-consuming but necessary activities. You might name your business the "Home-delivered Gourmet" or something similar. Print up flyers offering excellent meals prepared and delivered, and distribute it in upscale new developments likely to house two-income families. Mention that they can have the speed and convenience of pizza delivery or frozen dinners but with the nutrition and taste of home-cooked meals. Locate ten families interested in your service one night per week, charge them the price of two pizzas (fifteen to twenty dollars) and you can easily earn two hundred dollars extra per week. Best of all, your only up-front investment will be the cost of printing the flyers and buying additional groceries.

When it comes to service industries, no idea is too outlandish. I recently heard of a woman who is a professional "stander in line"—that's right, she stands in lines for a very handsome hourly rate. If someone can make money standing in line, I bet your idea will fly, too.

Jinny Grisolia: Service With a Smile

In July 1986, Jinny Grisolia said good-bye to thirteen years of government work to start her own day-care center. The general consensus among her co-workers was that her business venture would never succeed. But all the skepticism in the world can't stop a woman with a dream!

Jinny realized she and her husband, Frank, who was supporting three children from a previous marriage, would never be able to afford a home unless she went into business for herself. She insists she never had a doubt about her endeavor, thanks in large part to the support and encouragement of her husband. She believed it would work, and if it didn't, then she would try something else.

At the time, she was living on the third floor of an apartment building owned by her aunt. Aware of the tremendous need for quality child care, Jinny persuaded her aunt to convert the first two floors of the building into a school. The two have been fifty-fifty partners in Precious Moments Preschool and Day-Care Center ever since.

However, the road to Precious Moments was rocky, to say the least. When Jinny asked the local zoning commission to allow her to operate in a residential area, they turned her down. After six months in court, she finally received the go-ahead to start the center. But, needless to say, the local authorities were less than enthusiastic in assisting someone who had taken them to court—and won.

Aside from the zoning difficulties, Jinny was amazed at how many state and federal requirements had to be met: special fire walls, a sprinkler system, bathroom facilities, and on and on. All of this, of course, cost money. But when Jinny went to the bank to apply for a thirty-thousand-dollar business loan, they told her to forget it! By her own admission, Jinny had absolutely no collateral of any kind. Fortunately, her aunt was willing to put up her house as collateral and they eventually managed to get loans totaling twenty-four thousand dollars from two separate banks.

Unfortunately, they spent every penny of it on renovations before they even opened. As a result, the first year was very difficult financially. In fact, Jinny not only didn't receive a salary, she was eight hundred dollars short of meeting her business expenses each month. Thanks to the volunteer work of many family members, they managed to make it through.

Eight kids showed up on opening day in September 1986. Since that time, the school has mushroomed, peaking at an enrollment of ninety students in

1988. Jinny now has four full-time and five part-time employees. The dramatic growth of the school is a credit to Jinny's determination to make Precious Moments a warm and loving environment.

One of the most gratifying moments for Jinny was the day she and her husband purchased the home that once seemed an impossible dream. "Even though Frank doesn't really express it, I know he's relieved he doesn't have to worry about how we're going to make ends meet," Jinny says. "I've been able to take some of the stress and responsibility off his shoulders, and that feels great."

Jinny can identify with the challenge of balancing home and business, even though her three stepchildren come only for the weekends. In the beginning, she worked twelve hours per day, five days a week. "I look back on it now and say, 'How did I do it?' But I did. I managed to get everything done, but don't ask me how. Now I work only three days a week."

According to Jinny, operating a service-oriented business has provided unexpected rewards. Her day-care center has brought Jinny into contact with children and families whom she otherwise would never have been able to influence. "Close to 50 percent of the children in our school come from single-parent families, and we have quite a few who live with Dad, only because Mom doesn't want the responsibility," she says. "Whenever I talk to parents about their kids, whether it's good or bad, I try to show them kindness and gentleness. I try to be a reflection of Jesus in the way I act. It feels good to know I can influence the children who come to our center. In that way, this business is also a ministry."

CHAPTER FOURTEEN

Direct Sales

Direct sales is a 7.5-billion-dollar industry employing an estimated four million Americans, 80 percent of whom are women (*Women Working at Home*, WWH Press, 1983). Sales is a field in which women have consistently excelled. Why? Because success in sales is a result of hard work and building relationships—two things at which women are particularly good.

Direct sales also allows you to set your own hours and career pace, and in many cases, be your own boss. Often, work can be done in the evening, when your husband or friends are available to watch the children. If delivering products is part of your job, no one will mind if you bring the children along.

Two major avenues of direct sales exist: person-to-person and party plan, which involves having a group of people gather at someone's home. Your personality determines which is right for you. Some people are too intimidated to speak in front of a group and would rather relate to people individually. Others find the party plan less stressful emotionally, because if one person isn't interested in your products, others in the group will help soften the blow.

The key to successful direct sales is choosing a company and product line you believe in and feel good about representing. Ask yourself these questions:

1. Does the company have a good reputation?
2. Do they offer employee benefits?
3. Are there advancement opportunities?
4. Is an up-front investment required?
5. Do you have to purchase a starter kit?
6. Will they provide training?
7. Are the products high quality?
8. Is it a legitimate business or an illegal pyramid scheme?

You should also consider how the products are delivered. In some instances, you have to deliver the products personally (Avon); other companies ship directly to the customer (Discovery Toys). One method is not necessarily better than another; there are advantages and disadvantages to each. Company delivery is more convenient for you, while personal delivery offers more sales opportunities. Again, it depends on your preference.

There are an estimated three to four hundred direct sales companies operating in the United States today, offering everything from toys and clothing to cleaning and health care products. Some are more reputable than others. If you are seriously considering joining an organization and have questions about credibility, contact the Direct Selling Association, 1730 M Street, NW, Suite 610, Washington, D.C. 20036.

Be particularly wary of companies that require a large investment or promise quick wealth. In this arena, the old adage is as true as ever: If it sounds too good to be true, it is. Also, watch out for any sales organization that stresses recruiting new members, rather than selling products. Such tactics often constitute an illegal pyramid scheme.

Olga Power: Filling Her Empty Nest With Merchandise

Put away that rocking chair. This sixty-two-year-old grandmother of sixteen is definitely *not* interested in sitting around. She conducts a busy and successful sales operation. But at first, it looked like finding her niche might be tough.

Olga Power dropped out of school after the ninth grade and took a job at a five-and-dime store. Not long afterward, she married and began raising a family. She recalls those days: "When you're raising eight kids, you're so busy all the time that you don't even realize how busy you are. Until it stops." Today, all of her children are grown. She describes the empty-nest syndrome as a "traumatic" experience. "I poured my life into those children for years, and when they were gone I went through a time when I didn't know what to do with myself." She decided to fill her days with work.

Initially, Olga felt her career options were very limited, because she lacked formal education. She tried cashiering jobs — after forty-plus years of mothering, she knew she could count change. But the pay was low and the working conditions were even worse. She then tried turning her love of crafts into a business venture and was moderately successful. However, it wasn't until she found a job as a home demonstrator with House of Lloyd that she began to blossom.

One of the things Olga likes best about her work is meeting new people, and she meets all types. She says, "I've been in the homes of very wealthy people, and I've been in homes where they could barely afford to buy a bottle of soda for refreshments. It's been a fascinating experience." Mostly, she likes keeping busy. "I'm not just sitting home getting older and older," she says. "I'm keeping my mind active."

The fact that she can simultaneously Christmas shop is an added bonus. Once her selling season is over, she's free to do whatever she wants with the merchandise in her sales kit. These days, birthdays and anniversaries are all taken care of with last year's product line. Her children and grandchildren don't seem to mind!

She finds the party plan well-suited to her, because it's less threatening than one-on-one sales. There's always at least one person at every party who is genuinely interested in the merchandise, and she'll focus her sales effort there.

Finding customers has not been as much of a problem as she had initially anticipated. The first thing she did was call her children. Each of her four daughters booked a house party, and from there the parties just seemed to multiply.

Olga obviously enjoys what she does and feels she has the best of both worlds: the security of an employer and the independence of working for herself. The company unconditionally guarantees everything she sells, and she doesn't have to hassle with collecting money or making product deliveries.

She also likes working only when she wants to. But that doesn't mean she sits back and takes it easy. She consistently finishes first place in her sales district. What keeps her motivated? A dream vacation to Hawaii. The company offers a free trip to employees who achieve a certain sales level each year.

Olga attributes her success to a combination of "ambition and bullheaded-ness." She knew a lot of people thought she'd never make it, and that motivated her to keep going. Still, there are times when the last thing she wants to do is load up the car and travel to a stranger's house to sell merchandise. "But I get up and go anyway," she says. "Afterwards, I feel better about myself."

Although her family has been supportive, she takes her share of good-natured kidding. "I get a lot of teasing from my kids. I've been called Mrs. Lloyd by more than one person in my family." Her husband, Jack, also worries that she's too old to work. But she insists: "I'm not going to let myself be an old lady. I'm going to keep working as long as God gives me strength."

CHAPTER FIFTEEN

Word Processing

Home-based word processing businesses are springing up all over the place these days—and for good reason. First, because many women have secretarial experience. Second, affordable computer systems make it easy to transfer skills obtained in the work place to a home-based business. And there is a great demand for it.

Many students, professors, job hunters, sales representatives, doctors, lawyers and insurance agents have need of secretarial support but not a full-time secretary. Offices with work overflow may also use secretarial services. If you possess secretarial skills and are interested in starting a home-based service, there are a number of excellent books that will show you exactly how to get started (see chapter 20).

While home-based word processors can make good money, there are disadvantages as well. You must be willing to work evenings and weekends, and many of your customers will need their work done *yesterday*. The nature of the business will require a lot of direct contact with the public, so you'll be expected to dress professionally.

The up-front investment can vary greatly, depending upon the equipment you purchase. Wendy Brooks (featured later in this chapter) spent five hundred dollars to launch her typing service with a used typewriter, but that was almost ten years ago. Donna Agnello, who went into business just two years ago, invested nearly ten thousand dollars to purchase state-of-the-art equipment.

In today's competitive market, a computer and letter-quality printer are virtually mandatory. In addition, you may eventually want to purchase transcription, fax and photocopy machines.

Unless you have a solid secretarial background, a career in word processing is probably not right for you. You will need to be familiar with various letter formats, type styles and general office procedures. For maximum efficiency, it is also vital to know your software package extremely well.

Wendy Brooks: Moving Beyond Home

For fifteen years, Wendy Brooks was someone's secretary. Today, she's the boss. She is the founder of Brooks Office Services, which provides typing, photocopying and fax transmission services for local businesspeople, students and anyone else who happens to stop in her storefront business. The company also provides permanent and temporary job-placement services, as well as word processing classes.

It wasn't until her two children were in high school that Wendy opted to start a home-based business. She had been enduring a long commute for four years and was fed up with the pressure and wasted time. Realizing all those traffic hours could be utilized more productively, she decided to convert her recreation room into an office and go into business for herself. With a five-hundred-dollar loan from her mother she bought a used desk and typewriter, wrote a detailed business plan and was open for business within two weeks.

Wendy's equipment may have been secondhand, but her service was first-class from the beginning. She realized that if she wanted to be considered a professional, she had to look professional. As a result, she woke up every morning at seven and got dressed (right down to stockings and pumps), just as she would have if she were still working in an office. She recalls, "Some of the people who used my service were businessmen, and a lot of them came to my door in business suits. They didn't want to be greeted by someone in shorts or sweats."

Wendy was equally serious about her business conduct. She reported for work in her home office every day, rain or shine, just as she would have if she weren't the boss. Some people, especially some family members, thought this type of self-discipline was a bit excessive. But there can be no doubt that her efforts have paid off. In fact, she credits her success in large measure to that self-discipline and determination.

Wendy feels her business success has affected the way her family views her. Even though her kids are older now (ages 18 and 20), she senses that her business has been an inspiration to them. Her husband's initial reaction was to let her get it out of her system. Now he takes it seriously. "I've heard him refer to it as *our* business," she says. "I even once heard him say *my* business, and I said, 'Wait a minute! I can live with the *our* business, but I can't live with the *your* business!' "

Wendy feels her career has strengthened her marriage because there's more emphasis on teamwork now. Her husband has become involved with her business and helps out around the house. "Whoever gets home first cooks," Wendy says. "Whoever has strength after the meal does the dishes. Nobody's keeping score."

As for her household, she says it's as organized as it needs to be. "I used to spend too much time worrying about nit-picky little things," she says. "It was just because I had nothing better to do. When you devote time to your business, some other things, like housework, have to be let go. And guess what? The sun still rises the next day, and no one gets any incurable diseases."

Wendy never intended to become an overnight sensation, preferring instead to build her company gradually, making sure the foundations were secure. Nevertheless, growth has come at an average of 50 percent per year.

The hardest step for Wendy was moving the business out of her home. When her operation grew to the point that she had an average of six to ten people coming to her house every day, some of them late at night, she knew something had to give. Although the neighbors didn't say anything about the disruption to their quiet residential street, she knew it wasn't fair to them.

The heavy volume of traffic through the house (there was no separate business entrance) was also taking its toll on her family life. Wendy realized she had two options: deliberately scale back the business by eliminating clients or move to an office.

She decided to go full-speed ahead, but the decision didn't come lightly. When the business was in the privacy of her own home, it was much less intimidating. If it didn't work out, she could always quit. But opening up shop on main street was a different story altogether. "The scariest thing was hanging up the sign 'Coming Soon' because I was saying to the world, 'I'm here. I'm taking a chance.'"

Taking that chance has paid off. Today, Brooks Office Services has over one hundred clients serviced by a staff of six. Wendy's placement service is doing very well. For the temporary secretarial service, she maintains a pool of ten to fifteen secretaries, in addition to finding permanent jobs for about two dozen secretaries a year. Now Wendy is considering opening a school to train legal and medical secretaries.

The business is not the only thing growing. Wendy is growing personally, as well. This fall, she'll be attending college for the first time. She plans to study business management and marketing. But Wendy is surprisingly modest about her success. "I really don't believe I have any more going for me than anyone else does," she says. "I think if anything I just have stick-to-itiveness."

She also has a philosophy emblazoned on her office wall: "Whatever you vividly imagine, ardently desire, sincerely believe, and enthusiastically act upon, must inevitably come to pass." That's a powerful recipe for success.

CHAPTER SIXTEEN

A New Era for Women Entrepreneurs

Women entrepreneurs are one of the fastest-growing segments of American business today. The array of opportunities available are as diverse as the women themselves. But one thing is certain, women in massive numbers are moving into the ranks of entrepreneurs. According to the United States Small Business Administration, by the year 2000 approximately 50 percent of all self-employed entrepreneurs will be women.

What is an entrepreneur? Someone with a vision for a new product or service, and the courage to make it a reality. Opportunities abound for those who are creative enough to offer solutions to the problems faced by Americans today. In our fast-paced society, people are crying out for assistance in managing the many facets of their complex lives. They want personal and professional services: child care, health care, home care, yard care, car care—every kind of care! If you can provide a needed service, there's a place for you in today's market.

Of course, no one loves gadgets more than Americans. If you can come up with a product to help people organize their closets, entertain their children or spruce up their yard, there's bound to be someone willing to buy it.

If you have fashioned a device to solve a household problem, turn it into a product. Chances are, other people are faced with the same problem and would be willing to pay money to obtain your time-saving, aggravation-saving or space-saving solution.

Truly, the possibilities are only as limited as your imagination. Chapter 17 lists hundreds of ideas for a home-based business and no doubt another two hundred suggestions could have been included. All you need to do is pick an idea and run with it.

Rhonda Kanning-Anderson: Building on Passion

There's no better way to build a business than with passion. If you believe strongly enough that people *need* your product, you're bound to succeed. Rhonda Kanning-Anderson is living proof.

In 1985, finances were tight for Rhonda and her family. Her husband, Mac, worked as a carpenter. Sometimes the hours were long and tiring; other times there was no work at all. To make matters worse, the Andersons could not get health insurance—a serious concern for a family raising four children in cold Montana winters.

Rhonda knew she needed to do something, yet she knew her children needed her at home. First, she tried baby-sitting. Unfortunately, repairing the damage caused to her house and furniture by the kids she watched actually cost more than she earned. Next she tried tole-painting children's furniture, but it was time-consuming and generated very little profit.

Not willing to give up on working at home, Rhonda and her husband purchased five acres of land to subdivide. Rhonda handled all aspects of dividing and selling the lots. In addition to selling the land, the Andersons built some of the homes. That arrangement worked well until the real estate market crashed in 1984.

It wasn't until January 1987 that Rhonda finally found her niche. One afternoon, Rhonda's sister called her in a panic. The woman coordinating crafts for the MOPS (Mothers of Preschoolers) program had to cancel.

Rhonda agreed to spend an hour showing the ladies how to organize an attractive scrapbook photo album, combining pictures, momentos, report cards, crafts, etc. Rhonda felt strongly about the importance of building family togetherness through scrapbooks. She wanted to convey how much it encouraged and strengthened her family.

Rhonda spent the next three days preparing. She analyzed how she put together her scrapbooks and why they were better than regular photo albums. She prepared a handout, explaining why family scrapbooks are important because they build self-esteem and preserve family history.

The response from the MOPS group was overwhelming. After the meeting, the women flooded Rhonda with questions. They also placed orders for forty scrapbook photo albums. (The albums were not available in stores, so Rhonda agreed to coordinate the order.) Rhonda recalls, "I thought *everyone* preserved their family photos as carefully as I did. My mother always made scrapbooks, and I just naturally continued the tradition. To me, it wasn't a big deal."

But to others it was a big deal. Soon Rhonda's neighbors wanted to host scrapbook parties. Rhonda realized that most people collect photographs for years, without ever organizing them. And few people know that most photo albums contain chemicals that gradually destroy photographs.

Rhonda knew she was on to a home-based business with real potential. She began to invest time and money in her new venture, called Shoebox to Showcase.

Rhonda called every church and civic group in the area, offering to present her idea. Not every group agreed to host a gathering, but many did. Over the next few months, Rhonda explained the joys of scrapbook photo albums to hundreds of people.

Her efforts quickly resulted in numerous scrapbook orders. Then an event occurred that changed the course of Rhonda's business. She received a notice from the manufacturer that supplied her with photo albums saying it was dropping the line of albums. Rhonda immediately called the company, fearing they wouldn't deliver her scrapbooks.

Cheryl Lightle, vice president of Webway, Inc., answered Rhonda's call. When Rhonda described Shoebox to Showcase, Cheryl found the concept intriguing. Eventually, Webway invited Rhonda to present her business idea to the company.

In March 1987, Rhonda met with Webway executives. Although not ready to make a commitment, the company was impressed with her idea. Encouraged by the response, she ordered business cards and bought new professional-looking clothes. She bought a van to haul her inventory and painted "Shoebox to Showcase" on the side. Then she bought a computer to keep track of everything. In all, Rhonda invested fifteen thousand dollars, money originally intended for a down payment on a house. Rhonda quickly ordered a thousand more albums and sold them within four months.

That *really* got Webway's attention. In June 1987, they invited Rhonda to meet with them again. This time Rhonda had solid statistics to back her convictions. Thanks to her computer, she had kept meticulous records, proving the success of her sales approach.

After five days of meetings, Rhonda signed an agreement with Webway, which would provide her with products and marketing material. Rhonda agreed to work as a consultant, paid hourly, to promote Shoebox to Showcase nationwide.

Rhonda recommended that the business should continue using informal workshops. She believed organizing a scrapbook should be fun, not a chore. She also noticed that the workshop format improved sales.

There was just one problem. Rhonda could be only in one place at a time, yet the demand for the workshops continued to grow. In 1988, Rhonda signed on eight consultants to help her promote the business. She encouraged them to conduct their own workshops and recruit new consultants. No longer a one-woman enterprise, Shoebox to Showcase became a multilevel marketing company.

The turning point for Shoebox to Showcase came when Rhonda appeared in *Focus on the Family* magazine and on the radio broadcast. "The response was excellent," Rhonda recalls. "We heard from eight thousand people. As a result, we grew from two hundred to eight hundred consultants in just a few short months."

Today, Shoebox to Showcase has twelve hundred consultants across the United States and Canada. Rhonda recently resigned from direct selling and recruiting to devote herself to training and encouraging her sales consultants. By any measure, Shoebox to Showcase is an astonishing success. In 1991, the company reached two million dollars in sales.

Rhonda is both thrilled and surprised by the success of Shoebox to Showcase. What began as a hobby, then a small home-based enterprise, has grown into a multimillion dollar corporation.

Part Four

LAUNCHING YOUR BUSINESS

CHAPTER SEVENTEEN

Hundreds of Things You Can Do From Home

I t is important to distinguish between working *at* home and working *from* home. There are few jobs that can be done completely at home, such as day-care provider or telemarketer. Keep in mind that even a mail-order specialist must make trips to the office-supply store, print shop and post office.

On the other hand, almost any job can be *based* at home—that is, home serves as your base of operations. A manufacturer's representative obviously must leave her own home to call on prospective buyers. But she can certainly make phone calls, write correspondence and complete paperwork at home, rather than at a downtown office.

It is also important to be realistic about how much money you can potentially earn, based on the business you choose. Some of the jobs listed here can only supplement your income. For example, it would be difficult to support a family of four as a manicurist. Others, such as an accountant or lawyer, represent a full-time commitment and may require years of training. The important thing is to choose the opportunity that is right for you, based on your goals, needs, training and interests.

The Possibilities

Following is a list of possibilities you may want to consider for your home-based business. Read through the list quickly and mark anything that grabs your attention. Then go through a second time with a more critical eye and begin to narrow down the list to about five choices. Rank them in order of preference and begin to explore each one in turn. *That means going to the library to do research, evaluating the market in your area and weighing the various factors discussed in chapter 6* (under the subheading "What Business Is Right for You?").

Remember, the best approach is to try one option after another until you find the right one (do give each your best shot). Don't give up if you discover that a zoning regulation or some other obstacle prevents your first choice from materializing. If at first you don't succeed, try, try something else!

- Accountant
- Acting Instructor
- Advertising Agency
- Aerobics Instructor
- Animal Breeder
- Animal Boarding
- Animal Trainer
- Answering Service
- Antique Repair
- Antique Sales
- Apartment Finder
- Appliance Repair
- Aquarium Design
- Aquarium Installation
- Arts and Crafts Fair Promotion
- Art Rental
- Attorney Referral Service
- Auto Repair
- Baby Gift Basket Preparation
- Baby Bracelets and Accessories
- Baby Shoe Preserving
- Baking (for local restaurants or direct sale)
- Balloon Delivery Service
- Basket Weaving
- Beauty Salon
- Bed and Breakfast Proprietor
- Beekeeper
- Bicycle Sales and Repair
- Billing (prepare and mail invoices for other businesses)
- Birth Announcements (ceramic, pillows, etc.)
- Boarding House
- Bookbinding
- Bookkeeping
- Bridal Consultant and Wedding Planner
- Bridal Registry Service
- Business Appraiser

- Business Consultant
- Calligraphy (invitations, poems, Scripture verses)
- Cake Decorator
- Cake Decorating Instructor
- Camp and Nursery School Referral Service
- Canner
- Career Counselor
- Cartoon and Caricature Illustrator (from photographs or at events)
- Catering
- Ceramics (instructions, sales)
- Chair Caning
- Childbirth Educator
- Child Care Service
- Children's Birthday Party Organizer
- Children's Book Writer or Illustrator
- Clipping Service (cutting out newspaper and magazine articles for specific companies)
- Closet Organizing Service
- Clowning
- Coin Dealing
- Collating and Stapling Service
- College Financial Aid Consultant
- Color Analysis
- Commercial Artist
- Communications Consultant
- Computer Consultant
- Computer Instructor
- Computer Programmer
- Consignment Shop
- Consultant (in your field of expertise)
- Cooking Instructor
- Cookbook Writer
- Copywriter
- Costume Design and Sales
- CPR Instructor
- Craft Supply Sales
- Crafts Sales
- Crafts Instructor
- Credit and Debt Counselor
- Credit Report Service
- Curtain Making
- Dance Instructor
- Data Entry
- Data Processing Service
- Day-care or Baby-sitting Service
- Decoy Design and Sales
- Delivery Service
- Desktop Publishing
- Diaper Service
- Dictation Service
- Diet Consultant
- Dog Walking
- Doll (house, furniture, clothes) Design and Sales
- Doll Making
- Dressmaking and Alterations
- Driving Instructor
- Ear Piercing
- Earring Design and Sales
- Economic Advisor
- Editor
- Educational Consultant
- Electrician
- Employment Agency

- Escort Service for Children or Elderly
- Estate Appraiser and Liquidator
- Estate Planning
- Executive Search Firm
- Exercise Instructor
- Family Counselor
- Fashion Designer
- Financial Planning Consultant
- Flea Market Vendor
- Florist
- Flower Arranger
- Free-lance Writer
- Free-lance Artist
- Free-lance Commercial Artist
- Fruit Basket Preparation
- Fundraiser (for nonprofit organizations, corporations, etc.)
- Furniture Restoration
- Garage Sale Planner and Promotor
- Gardener
- Gift Basket Preparation
- Gift Buying and Wrapping
- Graphic Designer
- Greeting Card Writer
- Gymnastics Instructor
- Handbill Distribution
- Handpainted Clothing Maker
- Handwriting Analyst
- Handyperson
- Hairstyling
- Health and Fitness Consultant
- Home Demonstrator
- Home-Management Consultant
- Housekeeping Service

- House Painter (interior or exterior)
- How-To Book Writer
- Image Consultant
- Immigration and Naturalization Consultant
- Income Tax Preparation
- Insurance Agent
- Interior Decorator
- Investment Counselor
- Janitorial Service
- Jewelry Design
- Jewelry Repair
- Jewelry Sales
- Kitchen and Bathroom Planning
- Labor Relations
- Landscape Design
- Laundering and Ironing
- Lawn and Shrub Maintenance
- Locksmith
- Magician
- Mailing List Service
- Mail-Order Business
- Management Consultant
- Manicurist
- Marketing Consultant
- Market Researcher
- Marriage Counselor
- Medical Transcription
- Messenger Service
- Monogramming
- Musical Instrument Instructor
- Nanny Agency and Referral Service
- Needlework Design
- Needlework Framing

- Newsletter Publisher
- Newspaper Delivery
- Notereader-Scopist (for court reporters)
- Nursing (visiting nurse)
- Office Services (photocopying, fax transmission)
- Painter
- Paralegal
- Party Planner
- Payroll Preparation Service
- Pet Sitting
- Pet Transporting (to vet, airport, training school)
- Photographer (free-lance, weddings, babies, etc.)
- Photo Restoration
- Picture Framing
- Pillow Maker
- Plant Sales or Rental
- Play Group Organizer
- Pollster
- Portrait Painter
- Project Finisher (needlework, crafts)
- Proofreader
- Psychologist
- Public Opinion Analyst
- Public Relations Agency
- Public Speaking Coach
- Puppeteer
- Quilt Making
- Real Estate Appraiser
- Real Estate Sales
- Researcher (for writers, attorneys, media, professors)
- Residential Manager
- Resumé Service
- Retirement Planning Service
- Reunion Planner
- Roommate Matching Service
- Rubber Stamp Making
- Salesperson (Avon, Mary Kay, etc.)
- Self-Defense Trainer
- Seminar Lecturer
- Sewing Instructor
- Shopping Service (for shut-ins, elderly, etc.)
- Singing Telegrams
- Software Designer
- Software Manual Writer or Illustrator
- Speech Therapist
- Speech Writing
- Stenciling Service
- Stencil Design and Sales
- Stockbroker
- Tailor
- Talent Agent
- Tax Planning Consultant
- Telecommuter
- Telemarketing Specialist
- Telephone Book Delivery
- Ticket Agent
- Time-Management Consultant
- Tour Guide
- Tourist Host
- Toy Selling
- Toy Making
- Transcription
- Translator or Interpreter

- Travel Agent
- Trip Organizer
- Tutor
- Typesetter
- Typing Service
- Upholstery Repair
- Used Book Selling
- Vegetable Growing and Selling
- Video Recording
- Video Recording Instructor

- Videotape Editor
- Voice Instructor
- Wake-Up Call Service
- Wallpapering
- Wedding Coordinator-Consultant
- Wood Carving
- Word Processing Service
- Writing Service (advertising copy, brochures, flyers, articles, fillers, greeting cards)

CHAPTER EIGHTEEN

Business and Home Management Forms

O n the following pages are forms and charts you may photocopy or adapt for use in your home and business management. Feel free to pick and choose which of these suit your business, and tailor them to fit your need. Please note that Day Runner offers convenient packs of preprinted forms in many of the categories listed here. You can contact Day Runner at (609) 461-1058. Below is a list of the forms included in this chapter and some suggestions for getting the most out of them.

■ *Checklist for Getting Started*. Double check this list of things to do to get your business rolling.

■ *Business Resources*. Use these forms to keep track of the people who can make your business more successful—suppliers, freelancers, experts, etc.

■ *Children's Chore Chart*. You know your children best. Customize and put this to work for you.

■ *Customer Contact Log*. This vital form is to keep track of your conversations with your customers: what you promise to do for them, by what date and at what price. Using it faithfully will ensure that your customers *stay* customers.

■ *Conversation Log*. This will serve as the second page for both your Business Resources forms and your Customer Contact Log. Using this will preclude filling in redundant information requested on the first page.

■ *Daily Planner*. This form should be used each day to maximize your effectiveness. Before photocopying, fill in those items in your schedule that remain constant. That way, you won't need to write them over and over again each day.

■ *Expense Log*. Since you don't want to pay more taxes than you owe, be sure to carry this form with you and use it constantly. You can maintain one central expense log or keep a separate sheet for each client if you bill back at the end of each month. I recommend you transfer your expense information regularly into your journal or computer program. Do not allow twelve months of vital information to accumulate in your notebook.

■ *Grocery List*. Before photocopying this form, fill in products you frequently buy. Listing needed items throughout the week will help avoid extra trips to the store for forgotten groceries and supplies.

■ *Mileage Log*. Every time you drive on a business-related matter, be sure to note your mileage in your log. This will come in handy at tax time.

■ *Projects Worksheet*. This form will help you keep track of any special projects you may be working on.

■ *Prospect Tracking Log*. The next best thing to customers are prospects. Keep track of who you talk to, what transpires, and most importantly, when and how you should follow up.

■ *Quiet Time Worksheet*. Using this form will help you organize your Bible studies and glean truths from God's Word to apply to your life.

■ *Things To Do Today*. The busier you get, the more you'll understand the importance of this vital form.

■ *Time Inventory Chart*. This is the key to your all-important time tracking exercise. List up to thirty activities you frequently do each day, such as bathing and dressing the children, packing lunches, etc. I've included ten common activities to get you started. Once your numbering system is worked out, you can simply write the appropriate number in the corresponding time slot. (It's easier to plug in numbers than write out the activities each time.)

■ *Weekly Evaluation*. This form is especially helpful as you're starting up your business. It will serve as a guidepost for tracking progress. As you become busier and more efficient, you may find it less necessary.

Checklist for Getting Started

Date
Completed   **Task**

_____   Complete Skills and Interests Inventory to determine what
                business is right for you (page 51)

_____   Complete goal setting exercise (page 21)

_____   Check state, county and city zoning code restrictions

_____   Obtain necessary permits and licenses for operation

_____   Check deed or lease for any restrictions

_____   Discuss with neighbors if your business will involve any
                additional traffic, parking, noise, etc.

_____   Determine legal structure:
                ☐ Sole Proprietorship   ☐ Partnership   ☐ Corporation

_____   Complete necessary paperwork (trade name certificate, part-
                nership agreement or articles of incorporation, etc.)

_____   Develop a business plan (page 54)

_____   Develop a marketing plan

_____   Develop start-up and first-year operating budgets
                (pages 106-107)

_____   Set up your home office

_____   Set up a filing system

_____   Set up a record-keeping system

_____   Open a business checking account

_____   Apply for a loan, if warranted

_____   Meet with your insurance agent to determine if additional
                insurance is required

_____   If you will be hiring employees, apply for an employer
                identification number

_____   Register trademarks and logos

_____   Obtain business cards and stationery

_____   Develop and print a brochure

_____   Begin advertising

_____   Write and distribute a press release

Business Resources

Category: _____

Company Name: _____

Address: _____

_____

Contact Name: _____ Title: _____

Phone #: _____ Fax #:_____

Description of Products/Services Offered: _____

_____

_____

_____

_____

Conversation Log

Date	Key Discussion Points	Date for Follow-up

Children's Chore Chart

Week _____

Chore	Whose Job	Mon	Tues	Wed	Thurs	Fri	Sat

Customer Contact Log

Company Name: _____

Address: _____

_____

Contact Name: _____ Title: _____

Contact Name: _____ Title: _____

Personal Info: _____

_____

Phone #: _____ Fax #: _____

Customer History

Date Met: _____ Where: _____

How Introduced: _____

Conversation Log

Date	Key Discussion Points	Date for Follow-up

Conversation Log

Customer: _____

Page # _____

Date	Key Discussion Points	Date for Follow-up

Daily Planner

Date: _____

Time	Project	Completed
6:00 A		☐
7:00 A		☐
8:00 A		☐
9:00 A		☐
10:00 A		☐
11:00 A		☐
12:00 P		☐
1:00 P		☐
2:00 P		☐
3:00 P		☐
4:00 P		☐
5:00 P		☐
6:00 P		☐
7:00 P		☐
8:00 P		☐
9:00 P		☐
10:00 P		☐
11:00 P		☐

Today's #1 Goal: _____

Notes: _____

Expense Log

Client: _____

Date	Description	Amount
	Total	

Grocery List

Beverages	Bread
Rice/Noodles	Milk
Canned Food	Butter
Condiments	Eggs
_____	Juice
_____	Dairy Products:
_____	_____
_____	_____
_____	_____
Toothpaste	Hamburger
Deodorant	Chicken
Shampoo/Conditioner	Roast
Hairspray/Styling Gel	Other Meat:
Bath Soap/Face Soap	_____
Other Grooming Products:	_____
_____	_____
_____	_____
_____	_____
Dish Detergent	Cheese
Laundry Detergent	Lunchmeats:
Glass Cleaner	_____
_____	_____
	_____
Furniture Polish	_____
Other Cleaners:	_____
_____	Frozen Food:
_____	_____
_____	_____
Paper Towels	_____
Napkins	Fruits & Vegetables:
Tissues	_____
Toilet Paper	_____
_____	_____
_____	_____
Plastic Wrap	_____
Aluminum Foil	_____
Other Paper Products:	_____
_____	_____
_____	_____

This Week's Menu

	Breakfast	Lunch	Dinner
Sun.			
Mon.			
Tues.			
Wed.			
Thurs.			
Fri.			
Sat.			

Mileage Log

Date	Destination	Purpose	Start/End	Deduction

Prospect Tracking Log

Company Name: _____

Address: _____

_____

Contact Name: _____ Title: _____

Phone #: _____ Fax #: _____

How Contacted: _____ Date: _____

Comments:

_____

_____

_____

_____

_____

_____

Follow-up Contact

Date	Outcome	Next Step

Projects Worksheet

Idea: _____

_____

_____

_____

Objective: _____

_____

_____

_____

Pros: Cons:

_____   _____

_____   _____

_____   _____

_____   _____

_____   _____

_____   _____

People to Contact for Information or Assistance:

_____   _____

_____   _____

_____   _____

Action Plan

1. _____
2. _____
3. _____
4. _____
5. _____

Quiet Time Worksheet

Date: _____   Passage: _____

1. Summarize in a few sentences what the passage is about:
   _____
   _____
   _____
   _____

2. Is there an *example* for me to *follow*?
   _____
   _____
   _____
   _____

3. Is there an *error* I need to *avoid*?
   _____
   _____
   _____
   _____

4. Is there a *command* for me to *obey*?
   _____
   _____
   _____
   _____

5. Is there a *sin* I need to *forsake*?
   _____
   _____
   _____
   _____

6. What application of this passage can I make *today*?
   _____
   _____
   _____

Things To Do Today

Date: _____

Item	Completed

Business Priorities:

1. _____ ☐
2. _____ ☐
3. _____ ☐
4. _____ ☐
5. _____ ☐
6. _____ ☐
7. _____ ☐
8. _____ ☐
9. _____ ☐
10. _____ ☐

Family Priorities:

1. _____ ☐
2. _____ ☐
3. _____ ☐
4. _____ ☐
5. _____ ☐

Spiritual Priorities:

1. _____ ☐
2. _____ ☐
3. _____ ☐

Notes: _____
_____
_____

Time Inventory

Week of: _____

Time	Mon.	Tues.	Wed.	Thur.	Fri.	Sat.	Sun.	Activity
6:00								1. Spiritual
6:30								2. Reading
7:00								3. TV
7:30								4. Phone
8:00								5. Grooming
8:30								6. Meal Preparation
9:00								7. Eating
9:30								8. Dishes
10:00								9. Sleeping
10:30								10. Cleaning
11:00								11.
11:30								12.
12:00								13.
12:30								14.
1:00								15.
1:30								16.
2:00								17.
2:30								18.
3:00								19.
3:30								20.
4:00								21.
4:30								22.
5:00								23.
5:30								24.
6:00								25.
6:30								26.
7:00								27.
7:30								28.
8:00								29.
8:30								30.
9:00								
9:30								
10:00								
10:30								

Adapted from Michael LeBoeuf's *Working Smart: How to Accomplish More in Half the Time.*

Weekly Evaluation Worksheet

1. What did I study in my quiet times this week?
    _____
    _____
    _____

2. Which of my business and personal goals did I pursue?
    _____
    _____
    _____

3. Which of my goals did I fail to pursue?
    _____
    _____
    _____

4. Did I attend to the important or merely urgent?
    _____
    _____
    _____

5. Am I using my unique gifts to develop my business?
    _____
    _____
    _____

6. Am I spending time in my office each day?
    _____
    _____
    _____

7. How's my business going?
    _____
    _____
    _____

8. What specific goals do I have for the coming week?
    _____
    _____
    _____

CHAPTER NINETEEN

Resources Available to You

As you prepare to launch your business, you may feel anxiety about making such a big leap all by yourself. Even though you may be a sole proprietor, there are a multitude of government agencies, trade associations and private individuals available to help you along the way. Do not hesitate to reach out for assistance to any of the resources listed here.

Again, read this portion of the book with a pen in hand. Circle or highlight any suggested resources you feel are worth pursuing. Then be sure to follow up by placing a phone call or mailing a request for information.

U.S. Small Business Administration (SBA)

The Small Business Administration is an independent government agency established by Congress for the express purpose of assisting small businesses. There are over a hundred SBA offices throughout the country that provide loans, management advice, counseling, helpful brochures and more. Be sure to contact the one nearest you.

Small Business Development Centers (SBDCs)

SBDCs are sponsored by the SBA in partnership with state and local governments, educational institutions and the private sector. They are frequently affiliated with state colleges. SBDCs can provide you with counseling and training services for very modest fees (and often at no cost). There are over 500 SBDCs in 42 states.

Service Corps of Retired Executives (SCORE)

SCORE consists of over twelve thousand volunteer retired business executives who provide training and free management counseling to small businesses. SCORE is a great place to start since they will most likely be aware of many other resources available in your local area.

Pick up the phone and schedule an appointment with SCORE as soon as you have a business plan in mind.

Small Business Institute (SBI)

SBIs are located on approximately five hundred college campuses throughout the United States. They provide in-depth training and counseling to small business owners. Contact your area colleges to see if this service is available.

Small Business Answer Desk: 1 (800) 827-5722

The Answer Desk is operated by the SBA's Office of Advocacy. It is an excellent source for information concerning all aspects of running a small business. Especially helpful is the free Directory of Business Development Publications, one of which is bound to answer any question you might have. And best of all, it's free. You can call between 8:30 a.m. and 5:00 p.m. (EST), Monday through Friday. If you live in Washington, D.C., call 653-7561.

Department of Commerce, Office of Business Liaison (OBL)

OBL provides information on all business assistance programs available through federal agencies. You can obtain a complete listing by calling (202) 377-3176.

State and Local Agencies

State Economic Development Agencies

No matter which state you live in, most jobs are provided by small business owners. As a result, most states have agencies specifically designed to assist small businesses. These agencies can provide you with valuable information on the opportunities available within your state and the best types of businesses to start.

City or County Development Agencies

These exist for the same purposes as the State Development Agencies but are specifically concerned with their own jurisdiction.

Chambers of Commerce

Most cities, and even small towns, have a chamber of commerce that promotes local business activity. Your local chamber is an excellent source of information on business opportunities in your area and a great place to begin your networking.

Local Colleges

In addition to offering college-credit courses in a wide variety of business-related subjects such as finance, management, accounting and economics, many colleges offer low-cost business seminars to the community.

Local Library

There is a lot of helpful information at your local library, so take advantage of it. Libraries can be intimidating, but if you ask for assistance, most librarians are more than happy to be of service (particularly if you go during off-hours).

Associations

These organizations serve a wide variety of functions, not the least of which is to put you in touch with other individuals with similar interests. They sponsor seminars, luncheons and other meetings on local and national levels. They also publish books, magazines, newsletters and other literature containing valuable information as you seek to establish your new home business. Look through the list and contact any association related to your field of interest.

American Craft Council
72 Spring Street
New York, NY 10012
(212) 274-0630

American Society of Artists
P.O. Box 1326
Palatine, IL 60078
(312) 751-2500

American Society of Interior
   Designers
608 Massachussets Ave. N.E.
Washington, D.C. 20002
(202) 546-3480

American Society of Journalists &
   Authors
1501 Broadway, Suite 302
New York, NY 10036
(212) 997-0947

American Women's Economic
   Development Corp. (AWED)
641 Lexington, 9th Floor
New York, NY 10022
(800) 222-AWED
(212) 688-1900

American Yarn Spinners
   Association
Box 99
Gastonia, NC 28053
(704) 824-3522

Art and Antique Dealers League of
   America, Inc.
353 East 78th St., Suite 19-A
New York, NY 10021
(212) 879-7558

Direct Selling Association
1776 K St., Suite 600
Washington, D.C. 20036
(202) 293-5760

Graphic Artists Guild
11 W. 20th St., 8th Floor
New York, NY 10011
(212) 463-7730

Handweavers Guild of America
120 Mountain Ave.
Bloomfield, CT 06002
(203) 242-3577

Homemakers Organization for
   Productive Enterprise (HOPE)
7172 Striker Road
Maineville, OH 45039
(513) 583-9839

Independent Computer Consultants
   Association
933 Gardenview Office Parkway
St. Louis, MO 63141
(800) GET-ICCA

Mothers' Home Business Network
P.O. Box 423
East Meadow, NY 11554
(516) 997-7394

National Association for the Cottage
  Industry
P.O. Box 14850
Chicago, IL 60614
(312) 472-8116

National Association for the Self-Employed
P.O. Box 612067
DFW Airport, TX 75261
(800) 232-NASE

National Association of Accountants
10 Paragon Dr.
Montvail, NJ 07645
(800) 638-4427

National Association of Secretarial
  Services
3637 Fourth Street North, Suite 330
St. Petersburg, FL 33704
(800) 237-1462

National Association of Women Business
  Owners
600 S. Federal St., Suite 400
Chicago, IL 60605
(312) 922-0465

National Chamber of Commerce for
  Women
Committee: Women in Home-Based
  Businesses
Ten Waterside Plaza, Suite 6H
New York, NY 10010
(212) 685-3454

National Needlework Association
650 Danbury Rd.
Ridgefield, CT 06877
(203) 431-8226

National Writers Club
1450 South Havana, Suite 620
Aurora, CO 80012
(303) 751-7844

Newsletter Publishers Association
1401 Wilson Blvd., Suite 207
Arlington, VA 22209
(703) 527-2333

Professional Photographers of
  America
1090 Executive Way
Des Plaines, IL 60018
(708) 299-8161

Public Relations Society of
  America
Information Center
33 Irving Pl.
New York, NY 10003
(212) 995-2230

Society of Craft Designers
6175 Barfield Rd., Suite 220
Atlanta, GA 30328
(404) 252-2454

Tourist House Association of
  America
R.D. 2
Box 355A
Greentown, PA 18426
(717) 676-3222

Newsletters and Magazines

Newsletters, often published by associations, can provide a wealth of information and inspiration right in your own mailbox each month. Generally, there is a modest annual fee for these. However, membership in certain associations will automatically entitle you to receive their newsletter. For further information, contact those that interest you and request a sample copy and subscription information.

Behind Small Business
Dona Risdall
P.O. Box 37147
Minneapolis, MN 55431

The Business Writer
Lawrence Ragan Communications
407 S. Dearborn
Chicago, IL 60605

Cast On
The Knitting Guild of America
P.O. Box 1606
Knoxville, TN 37901

The Christian Communicator
Box 827
San Juan Capistrano, CA 92675

Craft Marketing News
P.O. Box 1541
Clifton, NJ 07015

The Crafts Report
700 Orange Street
Wilmington, DE 19899

Cross and Quill
Christian Writers Fellowship
  International
590 W. Mercers Fernery Rd.
DeLand, FL 32720

The Eggers Journal
(Egg Decorating)
525 Fisher Ave.
Box 419
Phillipsburg, NJ 08865

The Family Day Care Bulletin
725 15th St. NW
Suite 505
Washington, DC 20005

Home-based Entrepreneur
  Newsletter
J. Esters-Brown Publications
P.O. Box 19036
Chicago, IL 60619.

Home Sweet Home Magazine
P.O. Box 1254
Milton, Washington 98354

Homework: The Home Business
  Newsletter With a Christian
  Perspective (sample issue for $3)
P.O. Box 394
Dept. 2M
Simsbury, CT 06070

Homeworking Mothers
MHBN, P.O. Box 423
East Meadow, NY 11554

Keyboard Connection
P.O. Box 338
Dept. DP
Glen Carbon, IL 62034

Mind Your Own Business At Home
P.O. Box 14850
Chicago, IL 60614

National Flea Market Dealer
11565 Ridgewood Circle
Seminole, FL 33542.

National Home Business Report
Barbara Brabec Productions
P.O. Box 2137
Naperville, IL 60565

Telecommuting Review: The Gordon
  Report
Telespan Publishing Corporation
50 West Palm Street
Altadena, CA 91001

Sew Business
1515 Broadway
Suite 1407
New York, NY 10036

WP News
211 East Olive #210
Burbank, CA 91502

Writer's Digest
9933 Alliance Road
Cincinnati, OH 45242

CHAPTER TWENTY

Recommended Reading List

T he following is a list of books that may be helpful as you move ahead to establish your own home-based business. Some provide general information, but for the most part, the books are specific to a particular line of business (e.g., How to make money at crafts, typing, cooking, etc.).

Circle those of interest to you and take a trip to your local library. Some of the publishing companies listed are a bit obscure, so your librarian may have to requisition books not on hand. Don't be afraid to ask for assistance in locating a particular book.

General Interest

Davidson, Peter, *Earn Money At Home*, McGraw-Hill.

Faux, Marian, *Successful Free-Lancing*, St. Martin's Press.

Gillenwater, Susan and Virginia Dennis, *Extra Cash for Women*, Writer's Digest Books.

Kahn, Sharon and the Philip Lief Group, *101 Best Businesses to Start*, Doubleday and Company.

Levinson, Jay Conrad, *555 Ways to Earn Extra Money*, HR&W.

Lieberoff, Allen, *Climb Your Own Ladder—101 Home Businesses That Can Make You Wealthy*, Simon & Schuster.

O'Connor, Lindsey, *Working At Home: The Dream That's Becoming A Trend*, Harvest House.

Siposs, George G, *Cash In on Your Bright Ideas*, Universal Developments.

General Interest—Marketing and Sales

Hopkins, Tom, *How to Master the Art of Selling*, Warner Books.

LeBoeuf, Michael, *How to Win Customers and Keep Them For Life*, Berkley Books.

Levinson, Jay Conrad, *Guerilla Marketing*, Houghton Mifflin Co.

Phillips, Michael & Salli Rasberry, *Marketing Without Advertising—Creative Strategies for Small Business Success*, Nolo Press.

Stone, Bob, *Successful Direct Marketing Methods*, Crain Books.

Ziglar, Zig, *Secrets of Closing the Sale*, Berkley Books.

General Interest—Time Management

Hummel, Charles E, *Tyranny of the Urgent*, InterVarsity Press.

LeBoeuf, Michael, *Working Smart: How to Accomplish More in Half the Time*, McGraw Hill.

Ortlund, Ann, *Disciplines of the Beautiful Woman*, Word Books.

Accounting, Bookkeeping, Income Tax Preparation

Ellentuck, Albert B., *Leventhol and Horwath Small Business Tax Planning Guide*, Avon Books.

Hooper, W.E., *Bookkeeping for Beginners*, Beekman Publishers.

Antiques

Lai, Hothem, *Antiques—A Collector's Identification and Value Guide*, Books Americana, Inc.

Michael, George, *Basic Book of Antiques*, Arco Publishing, Inc.
Dorn, Silvia, *Insider's Guide to Antiques, Art and Collectibles*, Cornerstone
    Library.

Bed and Breakfasts

Rundback, Betty and Nancy Ackerman, *Bed and Breakfast USA: A Guide to
    Tourist Homes and Guest Houses*, E.P. Dutton.
Stankus, Jan, *How To Open & Operate a Bed & Breakfast Home*, The Globe
    Pequot Press.
Mathews, Beverly, *Start Your Own Bed & Breakfast Business*, Pocket Books.

Clipping Service

Smith, Demaris C., *Starting and Operating a Clipping Service*, Pilot Books.

Color Consulting

Eiseman, Leatrice, *Alive with Color: The Total Color System for Women and
    Men*, Acropolis Books, Ltd.
Jackson, Carol, *Color Me Beautiful*, Ballantine Books, Inc.

Consulting, General

Bermont, Hubert, *How to Become a Successful Consultant in Your Own
    Field*, Bermont Books.
Holtz, Herman, *How to Succeed as an Independent Consultant*, John Wiley
    & Sons, Inc.
Kelley, Robert E., *Consulting: The Complete Guide to a Profitable Career*,
    Charles Scribner's Sons.
Shenson, Howard L., *How to Create and Market a Successful Seminar or
    Workshop*, Bermont Books.
Shensen, Howard L., *How to Strategically Negotiate the Consulting Con-
    tract*, Bermont Books.
Shensen, Howard L., *The Successful Consultant's Guide to Fee Setting*,
    Bermont Books.

Catering and Cooking

Baker, Nancy C., *Cashing in on Cooking*, Contemporary Books.

Blanchard, Marjorie P., *Cater From Your Kitchen: Income From Your Home Business*, Bobbs-Merrill.

Harris, Catherine, *Cash From Your Kitchen*, Henry Holt & Company.

Howard, Alice, *Turn Your Kitchen into a Goldmine*, Harper and Row.

Shown, Janet, *Freelance Foodcrafting: How to Become Profitably Self-Employed in Your Own Creative Cooking Business*, Live Oak Publications.

Splaver, Bernard R., *Successful Catering*, CBI Publishing.

Stewart, Martha, *Entertaining*, Crown Publishers, Inc.

Sutherland, Douglas, *Professional Catering, Cookery & Kitchen Practice*, Trans-Atlantic Publications.

Terrell, Margaret, *Professional Food Preparation*, John Wiley & Sons, Inc.

Weiss, Hal and E. Weiss, *Catering Handbook*, Hayden Book Co.

Crafts

Brabec, Barbara, *Crafts: Marketing Success Secrets*, Betterway Publications.

Brabec, Barbara, *Creative Cash*, Betterway Publications.

Cornelius, Rosemary, Peg Doffek and Sue Hardy, *Teaching Needlecraft*, Van Nostrand Reinhold.

Hynes, William G., *Start & Run a Profitable Craft Business*, ISC Press.

Long, Steve and Cindy, *You Can Make Money From Your Arts and Crafts*, Mark Publishing.

Isenberg, Anita and Seymour, *How to Work in Stained Glass*, Chilton Book Company.

Scott, Michael, *The Crafts Business Encyclopedia*, Harcourt Brace Jovanovich.

Sommer, Elyse, *Career Opportunities in Crafts*, Crown Publishers.

Day Care

Ashworth, Tanya, *Caring For Kids: A Concise Guide to Establish a Successful Day-Care Center*, Vade Mecum Press.

Gallagher, Patricia C., *Start Your Own At-Home Child Care Business*, Doubleday.

Squibb, Betsy, *Family Day Care*, Harvard Common Press.

Desktop Publishing and Computing

Bove, Tony and Cheryl Rhodes, *The Art of Desktop Publishing—Using the Personal Computer to Publish it Yourself*, Bantam Books.

Cassell, Dana, *Making Money with your Home Computer*, Dodd Mead and Company.

Friedberg, Ardy, *Computer Freelancers Handbook: Moonlighting with Your Home Computer*, New American Library.

Hudson, Howard, *Publishing Newsletters*, Charles Scribners Sons.

McConnel, Patricia, *Women's Work-at-Home Handbook: Income and Independence with a Computer*, Bantam Books.

Entertainment

Elliott, Tom, *Clowns, Clients, and Chaos: Starting a Hometown Talent Agency for Fun and Profit*, TEP.

Flea Marketing

Miner, Robert G., *Flea Market Handbook*, Berkshire Traveller.

Franchising

Arden, Lynie, *Franchises You Can Run From Home*, John Wiley & Sons, Inc.

Instructional Services

Holt, Linda, *How to Start & Manage a Dance Fitness Business*, Strode.

Interior Design

Alderman, Robert, *How to Make More Money at Interior Design*, Van Nostrand Reinhold.

Jewelry

French, Bernada, *Jewelry Craft Made Easy*, Gembooks.

Geisinger, Iva, *Jewelry Maker's Handbook*, Gembooks.

Wiener, Louis, *Handmade Jewelry: A Manual of Techniqes*, Van Nostrand Reinhold.

Wykoff, Gerald L., *You Can Master Jewelry Design and Creation*, Adamas Publishers.

Mail Order

Cohen, William, *Building a Mail Order Business*, John Wiley & Sons, Inc.

Hoge, Cecil, *Mail Order Know-How*, Ten Speed Press.

Hoge, Cecil, *Mail Order Moonlighting*, Ten Speed Press.

Marden, Carol Kotsher, *Mothering and Managing a Mail Order Business at Home*, MHBN Publishing.

Powers, Melvin, *How to Get Rich in Mail Order*, Wilshire Book Co.

Simon, Julian L., *How to Start and Operate a Mail Order Business*, McGraw-Hill.

Photography

Duren, Lista and Billy McDonald, *Building Your Own Home Darkroom Step-by-Step*, Van Nostrand Reinhold.

Duren, Lista, *Frame It: A Complete Do-It-Yourself Guide to Picture Framing*, Houghton Mifflin Co.

Rosen, Frederic, *Professional Photographer's Business Guide,* Watson-Guptill.

Schwartz, Ted, *How to Be a Freelance Photographer*. Contemporary Books.

Werner, Mike and Carol, *How to Create and Sell Photo Products*, Writer's Digest Books.

Photographer's Market, Issued annually listing 2,500 photo buyers. Writer's Digest Books.

Telecommuting

Arden, Lynie, *The Work-At-Home Sourcebook*, Live Oak Publications.

Typing Service

Aliaga, Barbara, *How to Start and Run a Profitable Home Typing Business*, ISC Press.

Culp, Carla, *Mothering and Managing a Typing Service at Home*, Mothers' Home Business Network Publications.

Drouillard, Anne and William F. Keefe, *How to Earn $25,000 a Year or More Typing at Home*, Frederick Fell.

Glenn, Peggy, *Word Processing Profits At Home*, Aames-Allen Publishing Company.

Glenn, Peggy, *How To Start and Run a Successful Home Typing Business*, Aames-Allen Publishing Company.

Goodrich, Donna, *How to Set Up and Run a Successful Typing Service,* John Wiley & Sons, Inc.

Kozlow, S.G., *How To Start Your Own Secretarial Services Business at Home*, SK Publications.

Writing

Bly, Bob, *The Copywriter's Handbook*, Henry Holt & Co.

Bly, Bob, *Secrets of a Successful Freelance Writer*, Henry Holt & Co.

Duncan, Lois, *How to Write and Sell Your Personal Experiences*, Writer's Digest Books.

Emerson, Connie, *How To Make Money Writing Fillers*, Writer's Digest Books.

Newcomb, Duane, *A Complete Guide to Marketing Magazine Articles,* Writer's Digest Books.

Rees, Clair, *Profitable Part-Time Full-Time Freelancing*, Writer's Digest Books.

Seuling, Barbara, *How To Write A Children's Book and Get It Published*, Charles Scribner's Sons.

Shimberg, Elaine Fantle, *How to be a Successful Housewife Writer,* Writer's Digest Books.

Wilbur, L. Perry, *How to Write Articles That Sell*, John Wiley & Sons, Inc.

Writer's Market, Writer's Digest Books (published annually, this directory lists more than 4,000 magazine and book publishers).